Endorsements for *Lord, Help Me Pray for My Kids*

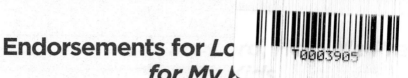

Knowing that my parents were praying for me had a profound impact on my life. Now I'm a parent, and I'm thankful that my friend Tony Wood has provided a way to help me continue being intentional in interceding on behalf of our kids. I believe this book will be a tremendous help to parents who lift up their kids every day.

MATTHEW WEST, Grammy-nominated and Dove Award–winning artist, and author of *The God Who Stays* and *Hello, My Name Is*

Tony Wood is one of the most prayerful and thoughtful people I've had the privilege to know and work with over the past decade. I'm grateful to call him a friend and thrilled to recommend this beautiful book of prayers for parents. As a busy working mom, this book is a godsend!

FRANCESCA BATTISTELLI, Grammy and Dove Award–winning artist

This book is a faithful guide in helping us cover our boys in prayer. It directs my wife and me with powerful, future-forming, difference-making prayers based on Tony Wood's insights.

TAUREN WELLS, Grammy-nominated and Dove Award–winning artist

Praying for your children is one of the most important things we can do as parents, and I'm living proof that those prayers work. *Lord, Help Me Pray for My Kids* is the perfect tool for parents who struggle to know how and what to pray.

ZACH WILLIAMS, Grammy and Dove Award–winning artist

Tony Wood has written a truly inspiring devotional. These daily prayers should be on the lips of every God-fearing parent as they face the challenges of raising Christ-centered children in today's humanistic, self-centered, self-absorbed culture.

JAY DEMARCUS, Founding member of Rascal Flatts and owner/CEO of Red Street Records

I typically prayed the same things every night over my little girl, yet these prayers from Tony Wood have changed the game for me. It's so exciting to pray the Word of God over my five-month-old and speak promises into her future. Run, don't walk, to grab your copy of *Lord, Help Me Pray for My Kids*!

TAYLOR CAIN MATZ of the American Music Award–nominated group CAIN

Lord, Help Me Pray for My Kids encourages us to fulfill one of the most important assignments we will ever have on this earth, which is to be spirit-led parents! Tony Wood has provided a powerful book of prayers that invite God to mold and shape, as well as protect and direct, our children.

JACKIE PATILLO, President of the Gospel Music Association

My friend Tony Wood has put beautiful words to the prayers I could not articulate for my own children. They are concise yet rich, and they are deeply felt as I pray them over my family.

DARREN MULLIGAN, lead vocalist of CURB/Word recording artists We Are Messengers

Tony Wood is an amazing friend and an even better family man. I can't think of a better gift to give your kids than entrusting them to the promises of God's Word through prayer.

TODD TILGHMAN, Winner of season eighteen of NBC's *The Voice* and author of *Every Little Win*

I fully believe in the power of prayer, and Tony Wood has beautifully crafted prayers that put words to my heart's desires for my children! I would suggest *Lord, Help Me Pray for My Kids* to anyone who longs to "pray without ceasing" for their loved ones.

TASHA LAYTON, Singer, songwriter, and BEC Recordings artist

Being a father is one of my most precious responsibilities. Songwriter Tony Wood uses his God-given talents to combine Scripture and his heartfelt testimony into an incredible daily devotional that reminds me how blessed I am to be a father—and, most important, how precious it is to have a heavenly Father. This is a must-read book!

JASON CRABB, Grammy and Dove Award–winning artist

Most people will never get the opportunity to write a song with Tony Wood, but having the ability to read his prayers for his children and then pray them for yours—well, that might be even better. I can't recommend this book of prayers, and the man who wrote them, enough.

CHRIS CLEVELAND of CURB/Word recording artists Stars Go Dim

I already pray over my daughters daily, but now I'm ready to dive deeper into my prayer life for them. I believe this book will be the nudge I need to become more of a prayer warrior for my children!

MIKEY HOWARD of BEC Recordings artists 7eventh Time Down

Tony Wood has done the work to give us words that put shape to our sometimes-inexpressible hopes and desires for our children. This book is a pathway to loving our kids better and a means of helping parents with the most important task we will ever have.

JOHN MAYS, Senior vice president of A&R with Centricity Music

When it comes to a book on prayer, only a true *prayer* who actually prays has anything to say. I know Tony Wood is a practitioner because I've watched and listened to him for twenty-six years. You will see, hear, and feel that, too, as you make Tony's prayers your own.

LLOYD SHADRACH, Cofounder and teaching pastor with Fellowship Bible Church in Brentwood, Tennessee

I love what my friend Tony Wood has put together! These daily prayers are a helpful tool to use in praying for our children with deeper intention, care, and a sense of surrender to God's will for their lives.

ETHAN HULSE, Grammy-nominated and Dove Award–winning songwriter

Tony Wood did what a writer is supposed to do—he put into words what most of us don't know how to say ourselves. If you want to pray for your kids but you're not sure what to say, *Lord, Help Me Pray for My Kids* is the perfect place to start.

BENJI COWART, Singer and Dove Award–winning songwriter

The passion and humility that Tony Wood brings to the prayers in this book are both powerful and inspiring. It's as beautiful as it is a peaceful read.

CINDY MORGAN, Singer, songwriter, and Dove Award–winning artist

If you listen to Christian radio, you have no doubt been impacted by Tony Wood's lyrics. He's a true wordsmith with a father's heart. How amazing it is to now hold some of those words in my hands and to pray them over my own family. This book will be on my bedside table.

KRISSY NORDHOFF, Grammy-nominated and Dove Award winning songwriter

With the general busyness of just *being* a parent, it's often hard to gather my thoughts when I sit down to pray. This book gives me a jumping off point and reminds me with every word that the top priority in our lives as Christian parents should be passing on a real and living faith in Jesus.

SHELLEY BREEN of Grammy-nominated and Dove Award–winning artists Point of Grace

If there were a required reading list for parents, I'd put this book at the top of it. Tony Wood's book is a daily gift to me as a dad by giving specific direction in praying for my children.

JONATHAN MASON, Vice president of Christian A&R and Publishing for CURB/Word Music Publishing

These simple prayers will transform the way you talk to God about your children. They helped me transform the way I pray for my own boys in ways that are real and practical. This book has also helped me put aside some of my own fears and anxieties about being a father. I highly recommend it!

MATT ARMSTRONG, Producer and songwriter with Chris Tomlin and Casting Crowns

Lord, Help Me Pray for My Kids by my friend Tony Wood is a treasure for any parent and their children. It is written with both wisdom from God's Word and with the heart of a parent. Tony is an incredible writer of songs, and now I have learned that he is simply a great writer!

MARK HARRIS, Pastor, songwriter, and founding member of Grammy-nominated and Dove Award–winning artists 4Him

One of the best gifts we can give our kids is to pray over them and guide them in God's truth. Tony Wood has given us a priceless tool for doing just that!

BRIAN WHITE, Artist, producer, worship leader, and Dove Award–winning songwriter

For years Tony Wood has used his incredible word skills to bless the world with hundreds of inspiring song lyrics. Now he uses those same skills to help parents who want to effectively pray for their children. This book is a great tool—highly recommended!

DAN DEAN of Dove Award–winning artists Phillips, Craig & Dean

This book is going on my nightstand! I love that these devotions start with Scripture, focus first and foremost on the attributes of God, then guide us in prayer for our children. It's a beautiful and vital resource for raising up the future of the church in our homes.

CHRISTY NOCKELS, Dove Award–nominated artist, worship leader, and host of *The Glorious in the Mundane* podcast

Lord, Help Me Pray for My Kids

365 Heartfelt Prayers for Parents

AWARD-WINNING SONGWRITER

Tony Wood

FOCUS
ON THE
FAMILY.

A Focus on the Family resource
published by Tyndale House Publishers

Lord, Help Me Pray for My Kids: 365 Heartfelt Prayers for Parents
© 2014, 2023 Tony Wood. All rights reserved.

Previously published as *A Parent's Book of Prayers*

A Focus on the Family book published by Tyndale House Publishers, Carol Stream, Illinois 60188

Focus on the Family and the accompanying logo and design are federally registered trademarks of Focus on the Family, 8605 Explorer Drive, Colorado Springs, CO 80920.

Tyndale and Tyndale's quill logo are registered trademarks of Tyndale House Ministries.

No part of this publication may be reproduced, stored in a retrieval system, or transmitted in any form or by any means—electronic, mechanical, photocopy, recording, or otherwise—without prior written permission of Focus on the Family.

Unless otherwise indicated, all Scripture quotations are taken from the Holman Christian Standard Bible,® copyright © 1999, 2000, 2002, 2003, 2009 by Holman Bible Publishers. Used by permission. Holman Christian Standard Bible,® Holman CSB,® and HCSB® are federally registered trademarks of Holman Bible Publishers. Scripture quotations marked NASB are taken from the (NASB®) New American Standard Bible,® copyright © 1960, 1971, 1977, 1995, 2020 by The Lockman Foundation. Used by permission. All rights reserved. www.lockman.org. Scripture quotations marked NIV are taken from the Holy Bible, *New International Version,® NIV.®* Copyright © 1973, 1978, 1984, 2011 by Biblica, Inc.® Used by permission. All rights reserved worldwide. Scripture quotations marked NKJV are taken from the New King James Version,® copyright © 1982 by Thomas Nelson. Used by permission. All rights reserved.

The use of material from or references to various websites does not imply endorsement of those sites in their entirety. Availability of websites and pages is subject to change without notice.

Cover and interior photograph of abstract mountain landscape (1929) by Paul Klee. Original from Yale University Art Gallery. Digitally enhanced by Rawpixel, public domain.

Cover design by Lindsey Bergsma

For information about special discounts for bulk purchases, please contact Tyndale House Publishers at csresponse@tyndale.com, or call 1-855-277-9400.

ISBN 978-1-64607-099-2

Printed in the United States of America

29	28	27	26	25	24	23
7	6	5	4	3	2	1

Pour out your heart like water
before the Lord's presence.
Lift up your hands to Him
for the lives of your children.

LAMENTATIONS 2:19

Introduction

No one can pray for your children better than you can.

No one knows their tendencies, habits, strengths, or weaknesses—in short, no one knows their hearts—like you do. I believe that the more specific we are when we pray, the more specific God is in responding.

I'm so grateful for the times I've spent praying with others. Their words have helped me express what was already on my heart but I hadn't found a way to articulate.

As I wrote these prayers—one for each day of the year plus a bonus prayer for leap year I pictured myself sitting one-on-one with family members, friends from church and work, my own children, and even strangers. I hope these prayers lead you to pray for your children on a number of topics you might not have considered before. I hope they will lead you to lift up your kids with a degree of regularity you may not have before.

If these prayers have any value, at best they are simply jump starters. If on some days you find yourself only a sentence or two in and then go off to the races with your own prayers, I call that *success*!

Thank you for allowing me the privilege of partnering with you in the holy pursuit of bringing your children before the throne of heaven.

May God be greatly glorified as we raise up a godly generation.

Tony Wood

Thank You

Terri—There is no one I know that I would rather have as a mother to my kids. You did it (and still do it) with great love, great wisdom, great passion, and with an incredible sense of what matters and what doesn't. The things I love most about each of our kids are reflections of you that I see in them. And now, killing it with the next generation! Love you.

Leslie, **Meredith**, **Erin**, and **Jordan**—I praise God continually for the privilege of getting to be your dad. I could not love each of you more or be more proud of how you live your lives and how differently yet authentically you each walk with the Lord. Releasing this book is a vulnerable thing for me. It's all the things I've been talking to God about since long before I ever saw you.

Justin, **Ben**, and **Ryan**—I feel blessed to call each of you my son-in-law. I have prayed these things about you from long before I ever met you, and you are God's answer to a number of my prayers.

Jack—You are pure golden sunshine in our lives. I cried tears of gratitude the first time I held your mom, and I cried tears of gratitude the first time I held you. Every prayer in this book is one I have prayed, adding your name in every line. I love you so much.

Caroline and Paige Wood, Austin and Vance Anderson, Ryan and Kyle Anderson (nieces and nephews)—I love you all, and these are the things I've been talking to God about since you were born.

Marty Wheeler (dad to Hannah), **Holly Zabka** (mom to Jacob, Houston, and Violet), and **Devon DeVries** (dad to Reegan and Rayf)—Getting this project out has been a *long* relay race, and each of you carried the baton for multiple laps before handing it off. I can't thank you enough for your friendship, belief, and partnership in ministry.

Dawn Woods—Thank you for the door of creativity you opened to me with this book. I will *never* forget the moment you said, "Well, let me get my calendar and see when we can release it." My world shook! I was thrilled . . . and terrified! Thank you for the opportunity, the friendship, and your belief in me.

Steve Johnson—I will always remember standing in the back of a music-video shoot with you—two guys with arms folded, killing time, and making small talk; two guys who really had nothing very creative to bring to that part of the process! Late in the afternoon I asked what you did, and you told me. Somewhere in the far-off distance, I could almost swear I heard a bell ring. In that moment I thought, *This is a moment of divine providence*. And it was! From your first phone message to every conversation along the way, I have felt your passion and belief in this project. Thank you. It is my deep joy to partner with you in this and to stand back and watch what God may choose to do with it in hearts and homes around the world.

Mark Harris—This book would not exist if you had not walked into my writing room one day and said, "Hey, I want to write a song about praying for our kids and the dreams they dream." So grateful for that song, but more for the friendship.

Zach Oswald—One day I told my wife that the joy was writing this book and the labor was typing it. It was killing me. The next week in the middle of writing a song, you leaned over and spoke "silhouette" into your MacBook. I had never seen dictation before. You changed my world that day!

Parenting: Guidance

Behold, children are a gift of the LORD,
The fruit of the womb is a reward.

PSALM 127:3, NASB

My God,

I will never forget those moments when I first looked into the faces of my precious children. Each moment was the end of a long journey of wild anticipation. And each was the beginning of another journey—quite possibly the deepest, richest, most trying, and most rewarding journeys of my life.

Still today, Father, as I consider Your goodness to me, I am overwhelmed with gratitude at the privilege of simply getting to be a parent. And with this great blessing comes great responsibility. I do not take it lightly.

Just as my children cry out when they have a need, hear me in this moment crying out that I need You. I need Your wisdom, I need Your strength, I need Your guidance. I want to be excellent at being a parent for my children. I realize my weakness, my inadequacy . . . and, most of all, my need for You.

Will You fill me, guide me, use me, lead me today?

Amen.

Salvation

You are saved by grace through faith,
and this is not from yourselves; it is God's gift.

EPHESIANS 2:8

Great Savior,

I will ask for many things on behalf of my children, yet I don't desire anything else as much as I want for them to have a saving relationship with You. No matter how deeply I long for this and no matter how passionately I request it for them, I can't make it happen. It comes only as a gift from You. Only You can turn a heart in repentance to You.

You have offered us the gift of Your grace through Your sacrificial death on the cross. Your Spirit is active in the world now, calling hearts to come to You in faith. I pray that at a young age, my children will hear Your Spirit calling to their hearts, and they will be convicted of their sin and convinced that no one comes to the Father except through You. May they place their faith in You. May they trust You as their Savior and Lord. Jesus, not only is Your grace a gift, but the faith to believe in You is also a gift.

Will You give my children the gift of faith to trust in You?

Amen.

Safety

Protect me, God, for I take refuge in You.

PSALM 16:1

Protector,

It would be unrealistic for me to ask that You keep my children from ever being hurt. Life in a fallen world means there will be bumps and bruises, cuts and scrapes. However, I do ask that You would protect my children from serious harm to their bodies, minds, spirits, and emotions. Will You keep them so close in Your care that no plan formed to hurt them can ever prosper?

This is a world of so many dangers, where news of accidents, disease, injuries, and evil is a daily part of life. This is a place where, as a parent, I could grow fearful, but I will choose to take every thought captive and rest in the knowledge that whatever comes against us must first pass through You.

So, Lord, wherever my children are, they are in Your hands. You are fully able to keep them safe and sheltered from harm. Will You please do that?

Amen.

God's Word

I am Yahweh your God,
who teaches you for your benefit,
who leads you in the way you should go.

ISAIAH 48:17

God Who Is Perfect Truth,

I pray that even at a young age, my children will have a special attraction to Your Word. May they somehow know deep within that the Bible is like no other book in the world. May that interest bloom into a passionate desire to know the truth on those pages.

May they respect Your Word. May they want to know Your Word. But most of all, may they obey Your Word, trusting that You indeed are the Source of all true wisdom and that You can lead them into better lives than they can ever hope to have apart from You.

Even today, Lord, would You increase their appetite for Scripture?

Amen.

Friends

A friend loves at all times.

PROVERBS 17:17

Jesus,

I pray that You would grant my children great discernment in choosing friends—especially in choosing their best friends. May there always be someone in every season of their lives who is that one trusted and trustworthy confidant. May these friends be people who also love You and desire to walk in faith and wisdom. Will You give them a blessed and special relationship that brings much joy and happiness as they encourage each other to continue in ways that are holy and right?

I know that along the way there will be friends who don't have a relationship with You. I ask that in these relationships, You would allow each of my children to be strong, a good influence, and a leader.

May my children never be companions of fools, as Your Word warns, but may they indeed walk with the wise.

May they honor You with their choices and in return know Your rich blessings in this area of their lives.

Amen.

Comparison

Each person should examine his own work,
and then he will have a reason for boasting in himself alone,
and not in respect to someone else.

GALATIANS 6:4

True Judge of All Things,

From a young age, my children, like everyone else, will begin to look around and compare themselves with others. They might be tempted to compare appearance, intellect, achievements, abilities, possessions, or relationships. Though I wish they wouldn't do it, I know that as they walk through a fallen world, they will.

Lord, I've seen how comparison can lead to pride, shame, and self-loathing—dark shadow lands for the mind to roam. From first-hand experience, I know that nothing destroys contentment like comparison. I pray that in those moments when my children are tempted to compare themselves, they instead cry out to You for a clear and right perspective. Would You meet them quickly in those moments with the light of truth that will drive back the darkness in their thinking? Will You return them to places of finding their contentment in relationship with You alone?

Amen.

Priorities

*What does it benefit a person
to gain the whole world,
and forfeit his soul?*

MARK 8:36, NASB

God above All,

This is a loud world that will constantly bombard and distract my children with things that are urgent, temporary, and ultimately insignificant. Many people foolishly live all of life in this place and never turn their attention to the things that truly matter. I pray that my children will live looking beyond the material things that are momentary and focus instead on the real riches of what matters eternally.

I ask that my children would not be seduced into pursuing lives of ease, comfort, and worldly acceptance. Instead, may they see the wisdom of laying aside their lives and their fleshly desires for the sake of the gospel and Your Kingdom. May they gladly wager their earthly lives and their eternal lives on the paradox that those who want to save their lives will lose them and those who lose their lives for You and for the gospel will find them.

Amen.

Siblings

How good and pleasant it is
when brothers live together in harmony!

PSALM 133:1

Father,

Some of the most influential relationships in our lives are those we have with our brothers and/or sisters. For my children, I ask that their relationships as siblings might be deep, loving, tender, and cherished. May they be true and faithful companions as they travel with each other through the journey of life.

Throughout this journey, misunderstandings, disagreements, and conflicts will continually arise. I pray that You will guide them to choose peace, love, and belief in one another. May they demonstrate grace and forgiveness and let no offense go untended or unresolved.

May they live in such a way that everyone will see that family matters most. Will You guard, guide, and protect their relationships as siblings and ultimately use them in each other's lives as a training ground for future relationships and for serving You?

Amen.

Confidence

Therefore, we may boldly say:

The Lord is my helper;
I will not be afraid.
What can man do to me?

HEBREWS 13:6

My Strength,

I ask today that my children would grow to display the quiet strength of character that is seen as confidence—not a confidence in their own abilities or anything that speaks of pride or arrogance, but that calm assurance based on the certainty of who You are. May they be so sure of Your love in their lives that it becomes a fortress wall against fear and the stumbling blocks that come their way.

May their confidence also come from knowing how much their family loves and cherishes them. May this be another layer of a rock-solid foundation for them to stand on when facing trials and testing.

Even today, Lord, will You move to plant this assurance deep in their hearts?

Amen.

Peer Pressure

My son, if sinners entice you,
don't be persuaded.

PROVERBS 1:10

Almighty,

Everyone has moments in life when a bad influence (sometimes from a good friend) tries to lead them into wrongdoing. My children are no exception. Lord, I ask that in those moments, my children would stand strong and choose to do the right thing, even if it means they must stand alone. Please give them strength of character to stand firm on their convictions of what is right and wrong.

May they resist the smooth words that entice them. May they recognize them as lies and press on in doing right.

May they know the blessing and joy of choosing to go Your way instead of going the way of the crowd. Please prepare them even now for those moments so that they will resist the pressure to do what is wrong and choose instead to do what is right. May You be glorified in their choices.

Amen.

Love

Love the Lord your God with all your heart,
with all your soul, and with all your strength.

DEUTERONOMY 6:5

My Loving Savior,

As my children grow, the diamond of their character and per-sonalities will begin to reveal itself more and more. Just as every jewel has many facets that display different windows of beauty, so will their personalities. Of all that You, I, or anyone else sees in my children, I ask that the most prominent and defining feature will be love for You.

God, I pray that my children's love for You will be fiery and pas-sionate and encompass all areas of their lives—their intellects, their emotions, their wills, and their physical abilities.

May their love show itself primarily in a strong obedience to You and Your Word. May my children love the things You love and hate the things You hate. This very day, may that love show itself in their lives.

Amen.

Humility

Do nothing out of rivalry or conceit,
but in humility consider others as
more important than yourselves.

PHILIPPIANS 2:3

Mighty King Who Came as a Servant,

You were truly the ultimate example of a servant. You fully restrained all power that was Yours and took the most humble position in daily life (washing the feet of Your disciples) and in saving us (submitting to an unjust death on the cross).

I pray that my children will love You and desire to follow Your example. May they constantly strive to live with humility and put to death any seeds of pride. May any evil seeds simply not take root or grow in the soil of my children's souls.

May they know success in the difficult battle of considering others as more important than themselves. May this play out in their relationships with other adults, with friends, and with their siblings. May my children experience the deep joy, peace, and blessing that comes to those who desire to model Your humility.

Amen.

Speech

Let no one despise your youth;
instead, you should be an example
to the believers in speech, in conduct,
in love, in faith, in purity.

1 TIMOTHY 4:12

Great Shepherd,

You know I desire for my children to be leaders and not follow-ers. Any hope of their becoming leaders hinges on their character and the example they set. I pray they would set examples of good-ness for others in the words they choose to speak.

I pray the overflow of their hearts would always be holy, pure, a blessing to You, and edifying to others. May their words be true, and may their lips be free from crass humor, swearing, slander, and demeaning and impure speech.

May love guide their language.

Amen

Disappointment

The LORD is the One who will go before you.
He will be with you; He will not leave you or forsake you.
Do not be afraid or discouraged.

DEUTERONOMY 31:8

God Who Is Our Comforter,

Like everyone else, my children will have to deal with people who disappoint them, plans that fall apart, and desires that are thwarted. When these events happen, I pray that You would send a good friend, a good song, or a passage from Your Word that reminds them of Your sovereignty over their lives. Remind them that You saw how these situations would play out ages ago. May this stir within them the confidence of knowing that You are leading their steps and that sometimes, from their vantage points, it may look as if life is falling apart, but from Your throne, it looks like life is falling into place.

Please meet them with confidence and comfort them in the assurance of Your presence, even in the midst of their frustrations. May they find peace in knowing not only that You go before them but also that You are close to them every moment along the way—even in the darkest hours of their discouragement. May Your nearness be a dawning that restores their hope and peace.

Amen.

Character of God: Immutable

I, the LORD, do not change.

MALACHI 3:6, NASB

Unchanging One,

You are immutable. You are the everlasting God with no beginning and no end. There was never a time when You were not, and there will never be a time when You will cease to be. There is never a change in who You are. You can never be any more or any less perfect than You are.

I pray that this truth about You will give my children great confidence in Your trustworthiness. As they live and grow in a world where everything apart from You is unstable and subject to change, may they find great strength and hope in believing that You do not and will never change.

May my children delight in knowing that Your plans are fixed, Your Word is sure, and Your will is always done.

Amen.

Contentment

Godliness with contentment is a great gain.

1 TIMOTHY 6:6

Our Sustainer,

You have made our hearts, and our hearts are satisfied only when they rest in You alone. Yet even as an adult who is also Your child, sometimes I rest in You . . . and sometimes I don't.

I know my children will face this same struggle. I pray that You will keep them from the love of money. Though this is a world that esteems those who attain it, may my children hold to a different value system and long for a different Kingdom. May they realize early that money is often like seawater—the more one drinks, the thirstier one gets.

May my children trust that You are sufficient for all their needs. Would You guide them to know You as their faithful Provider? May contentment be a cloak around them that brings great peace to their days.

Amen.

Faithfulness

Be faithful until death,
and I will give you the crown of life.

REVELATION 2:10

Faithful One,

Many people declare their intent to follow You. Some even start off strong but eventually abandon the narrow road of trust for an easier, less demanding broad road.

I pray that my children would be found faithful in finishing the race that is set before them. May they endeavor to remain loyal to You, and may they be diligent in pursuing You.

May their faithfulness to You be so undeniable that it earns them the respect of those they encounter.

Amen.

Our Home

The [LORD] . . . blesses the home of the righteous.

PROVERBS 3:33

Our Perfect Dwelling Place,

I think about the memories our family is making these days among the windows and walls that we call home—and the memories yet to come. Lord, a home is designed to be a safe harbor for hearts in a stormy, dangerous world. We want everything about our home to be pleasing to You.

May my children grow to love You more because of the time we spend as a family in this place. May these rooms be seen as places of grace, kindness, love, joy, and peace—everything that reflects Your presence.

We invite You to dwell mightily with us. Come fill these rooms.

Amen.

Prayer

Pray constantly.

1 THESSALONIANS 5:17

God Who Hears the Prayers of His Children,

May You often hear the voices of my children praying. I desire that they would learn that You are the God who longs for them to draw near and call on You. May my children be marked by the examples of those around them who are faithful pray-ers.

Lord, would You grow my children into regular pray-ers? May they have a time every day when they pour out their hearts to You.

May they also be spontaneous and persistent, bringing all their concerns before You because they know You care. Would You teach my children how to be diligent intercessors on behalf of others?

Even today, may their time with You be real and rich.

Amen.

Giftings

Based on the gift each one has received,
use it to serve others, as good managers
of the varied grace of God.

1 PETER 4:10

Gracious Giver of Gifts,

I know every parent believes their children are uniquely talented. In light of Your Word, I know that this is true of my children in a spiritual sense! Just as You created them with unique fingerprints, You also designed and wired them for service in Your body. From the beginning of time, You ordained them to do good works.

I pray that they would discover what their special gifts are and that they would be diligent to use them, remaining faithful in small things until You trust them with larger capacities of service. It will be my great joy to see the ways You plan to use my children's giftings for the benefit of Your church and for Your glory.

Amen.

Purity

Don't share in the sins of others.
Keep yourself pure.

1 TIMOTHY 5:22

Holy One,

Evidence abounds that purity is not a virtue this world esteems or celebrates. Yet in Your Kingdom, purity marks those who belong to You.

Lord, will You guard my children's minds so that the impurities they encounter will not stick or become regular parts of their thinking? Will You guard their hearts from the vices that would strive to take root? May the pattern of their lips be to speak only of things that are good and right and holy.

Would You impress on them the high value and incredible worth of sexual purity so that they will esteem it as You do? In moments when they are tested in this area, may they wisely flee from youthful lusts. May they serve You with purity in all their intents and actions.

Amen.

Encouragement

Encourage each other daily.

HEBREWS 3:13

Encourager of Our Souls,

Some people are always pleasant to be around. Something about their demeanors radiates hope, kindness, and encouragement to others. I pray that my children would be among those people!

May it be that others somehow simply feel better about themselves when they are around my children. May my kids always have something pleasant to say, and may their words leave others feeling cared for.

Since we never really know the difficulties those around us may be facing, would You speak words of encouragement through my children to those they meet along the way?

Amen.

Forgiveness

Forgive us our debts,
as we also have forgiven our debtors.

MATTHEW 6:12

Giver of Grace,

As children who were born in the aftermath of the Fall, we all are sinful and selfish and will naturally choose to go our own ways and not Yours. This sin of prideful rebellion is our greatest weakness and the biggest problem we all face.

I pray that as soon as possible, my children would comprehend the offer of Your incredible grace and cry out for You to forgive their sin. I know You will meet them in that moment with Your mercy and free them from the ultimate penalty of sin.

Though this will bring them into a right relationship with You, like everyone else, they will still fall short daily and need Your cleansing. May my children be faithful to cry out for Your forgiveness for the everyday offenses of their lives. May they know the sweet relief of Your pardon. In response, may they live with great grace for those who offend them.

Amen.

Habits

Since we also have such a large cloud
of witnesses surrounding us, let us lay aside
every weight and the sin that so easily ensnares us.

HEBREWS 12:1

Christ Who Set Us Free,

I have seen how a snowball, though small and insignificant, can roll down a hill and pick up a great amount of mass and weight. I'm aware that along the way of life, my children will pick up habits and ways of thinking and doing things.

Many of these habits will be good and useful, but negative habits can also take root and lead to difficult consequences down the line. These negative patterns can evolve and eventually hinder my children's walk with You.

Would You give me insight to recognize these patterns early on, and would You allow my children to have tender spirits toward making changes that would help them avoid being entangled in unwise habits? May they run the race of faith unencumbered and with great endurance.

Amen.

Wisdom

The one who walks with the wise will become wise,
but a companion of fools will suffer harm.

PROVERBS 13:20

Faithful Friend,

You have made clear in Your Word, and I have seen it happen in life, that those we associate with have power to shape our character. I pray that in all seasons of life, You would surround my children with wise, like-minded, like-hearted friends. May these friendships allow all of them to learn great things from one another and be encouraged to continue doing what is right.

What a joy for parents' hearts to see their children growing wiser because of the people they choose to be around.

May my children's friends bring out the best that is already in them, and even add good virtues to the ones that are already there.

Amen.

Kingdom-Minded

Seek first the kingdom of God and His righteousness,
and all these things [you need] will be provided for you.

MATTHEW 6:33

King of Kings,

These brains You have created within us are wondrous things. Even in times of rest, we are running down a hundred alleyways of thought. There is always something on our minds.

I pray that the chief concern of my children will be for You, Your glory, and Your Kingdom. This will always lead to a right perspective in so many situations and help establish their priorities. May thoughts of Your Kingdom always bring sweet contentment and rest.

Will You guard them from having an obsessive focus on lesser things, including food, clothing, and other pleasures? Instead, may they set their hopes and expectations on the eternal—a harbor safe from fear and worry. For Your high honor, our King.

Amen.

Listening

Everyone must be quick to hear,
slow to speak, and slow to anger.

JAMES 1:19

Voice of Truth,

You are always speaking. Your Word is waiting for us anytime we want to know Your heart and mind. I pray that my children would be driven to Your Word by all the events of life—the best and the worst. I ask that they would always want to know Your perspective and be quick to listen to Your voice.

In a world that values instant reactions to whatever news-worthy event is happening, I pray that in all situations, my children's responses would be careful and measured—given only after thoughtful consideration of what Your Holy Word says.

May their cautious responses also guard them from premature expressions of anger.

Amen.

Quarrels

Reject foolish and ignorant disputes,
knowing that they breed quarrels.

2 TIMOTHY 2:23

God of Peace,

My children will sometimes be around friends and others who obsess about petty things. These people will attempt to draw my children into foolish and unproductive speculations.

I ask that You would guide my kids with Your discernment in these moments, and may they be willing to not weigh in. May they instead recognize these fruitless discussions for what they are and know that they only lead to more quarreling and divisiveness.

May my children be at peace with simply walking away.

Amen.

Obedience

If you love Me, you will keep My commands.

JOHN 14:15

Most High God,

You know the desire of my heart is for my children to lead blessed lives. I believe this comes only from following You. I want to see my children obeying all You have commanded in Your Word. Yet I'm aware that some people give exterior appearances of obedience while simply masking hearts that desire to do otherwise. God, may this never be so with my children!

May their obedience come from a deep, passionate love for You and cause the riches of heaven to overflow into their earthly days.

May my children call You their Lord and gladly do what You say.

Amen.

Diligence

Go to the ant, you slacker!
Observe its ways and become wise.
Without leader, administrator, or ruler,
it prepares its provisions in summer;
it gathers its food during harvest.

PROVERBS 6:6-8

Ever-Working God,

Warnings against laziness abound in Your Word. It is a sure sign of disobedience to You and a disappointment to any parent.

God, I ask that Your Spirit and Your wisdom would stir deep within my children and be evident in their motivation. Would You instill in my children a vision and initiative for doing great things in all areas of their lives?

May this be evident in their schoolwork and learning. May it show in their approach to chores and work around the home. May they be especially motivated regarding spiritual pursuits.

Would You motivate them to regularly spend time in Your Word and in prayer even without outside influences?

Amen.

Choices

As for me and my family,
we will worship Yahweh.

JOSHUA 24:15

One True God,

O ageless King who reigns on heaven's throne, I look around and see so many people who have allowed something other than You to rule from the thrones of their lives. Regarding my household, we have made a choice: We love, serve, and live for You alone.

I pray that my children would clearly see the wisdom and blessing of this choice and, in response, would desire the same kind of relationship with You. May they courageously stand against the culture and boldly declare they belong to You.

You are worthy of our trust and allegiance.

Amen.

Anger

Be angry and do not sin. Don't let the sun go down
on your anger, and don't give the Devil an opportunity.

EPHESIANS 4:26-27

God of Joy and Justice,

Many times in my children's lives, situations will cause them to become angry. I pray that they will exercise the fruit of self-control and not respond in a hasty, unwise, and immature manner.

May they never allow their anger to go unchecked or unacknowledged. May anger never linger in their hearts. May anger never turn to bitterness, resentment, or self-righteousness.

Would You always prompt them to seek reconciliation with You and with those who have wronged them? May they always be tender to Your Spirit's leading.

Amen.

Discernment

*I pray this: that your love will keep on growing
in knowledge and every kind of discernment,
so that you can approve the things that are
superior and can be pure and blameless.*

PHILIPPIANS 1:9-10

All-Wise One,

There will always be some new spiritual trend or fad coming down the road. While they might appear to be new, most are really just a fresh coat of paint on some old half-truth or lie.

I pray that my children's discernment would be such that they can recognize ideas that conflict with Your revealed Word. May they never give time and consideration to any works-based religion but always only trust in the salvation that comes through faith in Jesus' atoning death alone.

May their discernment simply be an expression of the overflow of their love for Your Word.

Amen.

Generosity

Give, and it will be given to you; a good measure—
pressed down, shaken together, and running over—
will be poured into your lap. For with the measure
you use, it will be measured back to you.

LUKE 6:38

Generous Giver of Grace and All Blessings,

You know the desire of my heart is for every good blessing to come to my children. Just as I desire that You would be generous with them, I want them to demonstrate their ability to handle Your blessings by being generous toward other people.

May their hearts be moved by real needs, and may they not simply feel deeply and then do nothing, but may they take action and respond.

May my children be lavish in giving of their time, talents, and treasures to You and others.

Amen.

Humility

When pride comes, disgrace follows,
but with humility comes wisdom.

PROVERBS 11:2

Pure and Perfect One,

My children will learn some lessons the hard way. But if they are wise, they will learn other lessons from observing the mistakes that people around them make. I pray they will learn the truth about pride from watching others and not from having to experience it for themselves.

Pride happens on so many levels, great and small, but stumbling is the consistent result for those who persist in arrogance.

I pray that my children's humble hearts will keep them from experiencing Your severe discipline and being disgraced before others.

Amen.

Joy

If you keep My commands you will remain in My love,
just as I have kept My Father's commands and remain
in His love. I have spoken these things to you so that
My joy may be in you and your joy may be complete.

JOHN 15:10-11

My Lord,

You invite us to know intimacy with You. As You continue to teach us new depths of truth in Your Word, we marvel at Your wisdom, Your grace, Your goodness, and the beauty of Your gospel. Because we trust You and love You, we want to obey You. And as we obey You, we are filled with joy.

I desire for my children to be filled with this joy. May they find it by walking closely with You. Through their obedience, may they know intimate fellowship with You, which always results in the fullness of joy.

Amen.

Perseverance

A man who endures trials is blessed,
because when he passes the test he will receive
the crown of life that God has promised
to those who love Him.

JAMES 1:12

Almighty Giver of Strength,

At some point, my children will deal with difficult circumstances. They may encounter them in the neighborhood or in a
classroom. They may come from someone who dislikes or picks
on them. They may have a strained relationship with a teacher or
coach or someone their age.

In those times, Lord, help my children endure well. May they
respond with self-control to hurtful words. May they trust that You
are the God who sees and understands all things rightly. As much
as it is up to them, may they pursue peace.

Would You help them, over time, see the blessed reward that is
theirs when they persevere?

Amen.

Parents

Children, obey your parents as you would the Lord,
because this is right. Honor your father and mother,
which is the first commandment with a promise,
so that it may go well with you and that you
may have a long life in the land.

EPHESIANS 6:1-3

Our Father Who Is in Heaven,

In today's verses, I see two commands: obey and honor. These commands are intimately linked. Obedience refers to outward action. Honor refers to the inward heart attitude of desiring to do what is right in the first place.

May my children never be outwardly compliant and yet inwardly prideful or resentful. May they instead choose to honor their parents because they trust You and the wise pattern of authority and submission that You ordained.

May an attitude of submission and respect form a strong foundation that sets them up for success in other relationships that also require authority and submission. As my children pursue actions of obedience and hearts of honor, may You bless them with quality and quantity of life.

Amen.

Love

The fruit of the Spirit is love.

GALATIANS 5:22

Loving Savior,

The greatest evidence of Your dwelling in someone's life is that love flows from that person. We see how Your love is not simply good intentions and warm emotion; it's always active in doing whatever is best for someone else.

I pray that even today the fruit of love would be evident in my children's lives. May it be expressed in their relationships. May it spill over in their words. May it be clear, compelling, undeniable, and beautiful.

Amen.

Hope

Those who wait for the LORD
Will gain new strength;
They will mount up with wings like eagles,
They will run and not get tired,
They will walk and not become weary.

ISAIAH 40:31, NASB

Our Rock,

There will be times in my children's lives when faith will look like standing still and doing nothing. The situation may require them to remain where they are until You open a doorway or tell them to move toward the next place You are leading them.

These times can be difficult, and my children might be tempted to run ahead of Your plans for them. Or they might become discouraged and lose hope.

In those times, will You help them know the great wisdom found in simply being patient and trusting You? May they wait for You in faith and with the hope that You will bring them through. In times of trial, may they indeed find that You are the One who will renew them at the perfect time, with fresh strength for what they are called to face.

May Your faithfulness be their great hope in the waiting.

Amen.

Conformity

Do not be conformed to this age.

ROMANS 12:2

Holy One,

My children, long before they can ever recognize or articulate what it is, will feel this world trying to squeeze them into its mold. They will feel pressure to conform to current values and to accept whatever is popular or trendy.

The world will draw them toward things that are trendy, but would You lead them to love what is timeless? May they resist being shaped by the spirit of this age.

May they seek Your Spirit's leading in all areas related to fashion, entertainment, and language. May they seek Your heart and Your values.

Amen.

Reverence

Do not come closer. . . .
Remove the sandals from your feet, for the place
where you are standing is holy ground.

EXODUS 3:5

God of Abraham, Isaac, and Jacob,

I come today asking that my children would truly have a spirit of reverence in all things regarding You. May a sense of Your sovereignty and holiness affect how they approach You in prayer and worship. May it clearly color how they speak of You.

Please let them never draw near to You—in public or in private—in ways that would be flippant or disrespectful.

May they know Your awesome presence in such a powerful way that it leads them to tremble before You. May a holy fear, respect, and reverence capture their hearts.

Amen.

Patience

Therefore, God's chosen ones, holy and loved,
put on heartfelt compassion, kindness,
humility, gentleness, and patience.

COLOSSIANS 3:12

Our Patient Shepherd,

We bless You for the way You are so merciful in dealing with us. If not for Your patient endurance with us, no one would ever be saved.

I pray that my children would exhibit patience like You do, especially in dealing with difficult relationships. May they find peace in Your sovereignty, knowing that You see all moments they spend with those who are hard to deal with. May they trust that You know their hearts. May they learn to sit quietly in Your presence even in the waiting.

May their choice to embrace patience keep them from despair and from wrongly taking matters into their own hands.

Amen.

Poor in Spirit

The poor in spirit are blessed,
for the kingdom of heaven is theirs.

MATTHEW 5:3

God Who Hears the Cry of the Humble,

I pray that from a young age, my children would be sensitive to the gospel. May they easily believe and agree that all have sinned. In light of who You are, may they see themselves as lost, helpless, and hopeless apart from Your grace.

Would You help them see themselves as souls that are bankrupt before You—those who are truly "poor in spirit"? May they, in an absence of pride and with no way of saving themselves, cry out to You for mercy and salvation.

In giving up their own kingdoms, may they receive Yours.

Amen.

Friends of the Opposite Sex

I am a friend to all who fear You,
to those who keep Your precepts.

PSALM 119:63

Faithful Friend,

I come to You on this day in particular to lift up my children, asking that You would bless them with friends of the opposite sex. I pray that these friendships would be pure and holy and pleasing to You.

In a world that emphasizes romantic relationships, I ask that my children would be able to resist the pressure to prematurely engage in intimate relationships with those of the opposite sex. May they instead simply enjoy rich and rewarding friendships until the time You lead them into deeper, more mature, age appropriate relationships.

Amen.

Character of God: Omniscient

Before a word is on my tongue,
You know all about it, Lord.

PSALM 139:4

All-Knowing One,

You are omniscient. You know everything that has ever happened, everything that will happen, every possibility, every detail of every life on earth as well as in heaven and in hell. Nothing good or bad is hidden from You; not one thing is unknown or unnoticed.

I pray that this truth would be revealed in Your Word and would leave my children amazed. May it mark them with great comfort that You already intimately know them and all their deeds, thoughts, weaknesses, and struggles. May this, coupled with the truth of Your deep love for them, lead them into greater worship and wonder.

May Your omniscience give my children great peace, and may it be a sobering reality to know that they can never truly hide anything from You.

Amen.

God's Word

*All Scripture is inspired by God and is profitable
for teaching, for rebuking, for correcting, for training
in righteousness, so that the man of God may be
complete, equipped for every good work.*

2 TIMOTHY 3:16-17

Word of God,

I pray that even from a young age, my children would experience a special attraction to and respect for Your Word.

May they always trust Your Word to be sufficient for speaking truth into all areas of their lives. May it be a guide for how to be in a right relationship with You and with others. May it direct them in making good decisions. May it challenge and set before them a path of life that leads to incredible blessing. May it speak correction to them regarding any false doctrine they encounter or any sinful behaviors they commit. May it prepare them for every good work You have in store for them to do and help them discern Your will for their lives.

Would You lead my children to look at all areas of their lives through the lens of Your Word? However much they saturate their minds and hearts with it, may they always desire more.

Amen.

Integrity

May integrity and what is right
watch over me,
for I wait for You.

PSALM 25:21

Sustainer of the Upright,

Because of other people my children associate with, a cloud of suspicion may sometimes fall on them. Perhaps their friends will engage in wrong deeds, or my children may simply find themselves in the wrong place at the wrong time. I wish that it would not happen, but I realize that it probably will.

In those moments, Lord, may my children's good names and reputations come shining through. May they guard their integrity because of how it reflects on their families, but mostly because of how it reflects on You.

May they find peace and rest in those times when they are falsely accused, knowing that You always know the truth.

Amen.

Wise Choices

Whether you eat or drink,
or whatever you do,
do everything for God's glory.
1 CORINTHIANS 10:31

Worthy One,

I pray that my children would be passionate about You receiving glory. May they want You to be glorified in their every decision. May they seek Your leading and Your will for all relationships and areas of their lives.

Even in mundane, routine, and seemingly nonspiritual areas of life like eating and drinking, may they seek Your direction. May they make wise and healthy food choices. May they choose to refrain from excess. God, would You keep them free from any addiction so they may not be hindered in serving You? May their lives bear much fruit and bring You much glory.

Amen.

Freedom from Unforgiveness

A person's insight gives him patience,
and his virtue is to overlook an offense.

PROVERBS 19:11

Gracious King,

I pray that Your grace will permeate the lives of my children. May it be so evident in them that little offenses along the way will simply roll off their backs without much thought.

Would You guide my children to be slow to anger and quick to overlook the ways they have been offended?

May they not carry with them remembrances of past wrongs. Would You also allow their forgiveness to bring a sweet forgetfulness of the times when they were wronged? May they live free from the bondage of unforgiveness.

Amen.

Respect

Honor all people.

1 PETER 2:17, NASB

God of Honor,

I pray that my children would be known for displaying good manners. In a time when disrespect seems to be the norm on so many fronts, I ask that my children would take to heart Your call for us to treat others with respect.

May this posture clearly show in the way they treat all those in authority over them—parents, teachers, pastors, police, military and governmental leaders, as well as the elderly.

I ask that showing respect would come from hearts that see the value and worth of all people You have created.

Amen.

Dreams

I know the plans I have for you . . . for your welfare,
not for disaster, to give you a future and a hope.

JEREMIAH 29:11

Wonderful Counselor,

My children, on their own, could dream big dreams for their lives. I pray they won't do that. Instead, may they seek Your big dreams for their lives.

May they believe that You have uniquely gifted them for some areas of service. May they try different things along the way that help them clarify their giftings and grow in confidence as they express those gifts and abilities.

May they be willing to lay down their dreams on the altar of sacrifice. Through this act of surrender, would You help them clearly see the dreams that are from You?

May they know the great hope and the future You have for them in Your plans.

Amen.

Consequences

The good person obtains favor from the LORD,
but He condemns a man who schemes.

PROVERBS 12:2

Friend of Sinners,

Somewhere along the line, my children will likely encounter someone who is a sneaky type of kid. Many parents can never quite put their finger on why they don't trust that child, but it is sometimes a suspicion that is well earned.

I pray in those moments, Lord, that my children will exercise discernment when it comes to that other child. May they respond with wisdom and simply avoid people who cause trouble.

It sometimes takes a while, but troublesome kids almost always get exposed for who they are and for their lack of character and trustworthiness. May my children learn rich lessons and gain wisdom from observing the consequences that fall on others.

Amen.

Temptation

*No temptation has overtaken you except what is
common to humanity. God is faithful, and He will not
allow you to be tempted beyond what you are able,
but with the temptation He will also provide a way
of escape so that you are able to bear it.*

1 CORINTHIANS 10:13

Our Strength and Help in Times of Need,

I know that You will not tempt my children. You will, however, send trials their way. These trials will be times of testing and will actually be opportunities for them to show evidence of their faith and trust in You.

If they are not quick in declaring their dependence on You, it can open a door for the enemy to slip in and tempt them with something that could lead to serious failure.

I pray that my children would determine to persevere through each time of testing and use these trials to more fully trust in You, Your promises, and Your Word. May they cry out to You and find that You run to meet them, give them strength, and lead them through. May they repeatedly stand on the other side of a trial and give You glory for Your goodness and faithfulness.

Amen.

Forgiveness

Be compassionate and humble, not paying back
evil for evil or insult for insult but, on the contrary,
giving a blessing, since you were called for this,
so that you can inherit a blessing.

1 PETER 3:8-9

God of Grace and Glory,

We will never bear an offense or insult that compares to the offense You suffered when sinful humanity rejected You. Even in Your death, we see You speaking words of forgiveness to the soldiers who nailed You to the cross.

I pray that when my children are mistreated, they would not seek to retaliate. May they instead trust You as the One who judges all people and events perfectly.

I pray that instead of seeking to hurt others in return, they would choose to bless. May they first bless their offenders by forgiving them and then bless them by praying for their spiritual condition.

Amen.

Parenting: Guidance

Fathers, don't stir up anger in your children,
but bring them up in the training
and instruction of the Lord.

EPHESIANS 6:4

Holy Father,

You are always perfect in all the ways You deal with Your children. I want to reflect You in the way I parent.

Would You please give me wisdom and guide me to be firm, fair, and consistent in all the ways I train and discipline my children?

I do not want to exasperate them. I know one of the most common ways parents can do this is by overprotecting their children. Help me remember that I am raising my children to release them into the world. May I give them reasonable freedom to make their own choices and even to make mistakes they can learn from. Would You help them demonstrate maturity and responsibility in these moments? May I not smother and hover so that my children's spirits become resentful.

Amen.

Freedom from Fear

When I am afraid,
I will trust in You.
In God, whose word I praise,
in God I trust; I will not fear.
What can man do to me?

PSALM 56:3 4

Our Refuge,

This world is a frightening place. Yet so often in Your Word, Your followers are commanded to "fear not."

My children will feel fear at times and will need to make decisions about how to respond appropriately in difficult situations. In those moments, would You always meet them with wisdom and discernment?

At other times, they may feel the emotional rush of fear wash over them, and it is simply an attempt of the enemy to mislead them and cause them to question Your faithfulness, goodness, and trustworthiness. In those times, may they make the choice to have confidence in who You are and who You have revealed Yourself to be.

May they regularly experience their faith conquering their fear.

Amen.

Purity

The body is not for sexual immorality
but for the Lord, and the Lord for the body.

1 CORINTHIANS 6:13

Our Provider,

I pray that through Your Word, my children would have a godly view of sex. May they correctly understand that You created it and blessed it and that You are greatly pro-sex within the context of marriage.

Based on a biblical understanding of sexuality, may they desire the best You have for them. May they choose to abstain from sex until marriage. May they continually make wise decisions to guard their eyes, ears, and minds from media that would advocate and encourage a lack of self-control.

May my children never experience the pain, shame, and consequences of sex outside of marriage.

Even today, I lift up their future mates, asking that You would place the same hedge of protection around them.

Amen.

Change

*Jesus Christ is the same
yesterday, today, and forever.*

HEBREWS 13:8

Unchanging One,

Our greatest hope and comfort is always found in Your character. As my children mature, they will become aware that they were born into a world that is constantly changing. Because of the Fall, change is rarely for the good.

They will see changes take place on this planet—earthquakes, tornadoes, floods, and fires; disease and death; political uprisings and war.

I pray that Your unchanging nature and character would be precious to my children. May they find comfort in knowing that You, the Timeless and Eternal One, know them, hold them, have plans for them, and, most of all, love them.

Amen.

Anxiety

Casting all your care on Him,
because He cares about you.

1 PETER 5:7

Bearer of Our Burdens,

I want my children to develop strong prayer lives—not a once- or twice-daily appointed time to talk with You but a steady, ongoing, unending conversation throughout the day.

Having this trait will help them bring any and every immediate concern right to Your throne room. May my children be so confident in Your care and concern for them that they will tell You anything that causes questions or pain. May they give over to You all their discontent, discouragement, and despair.

May my children not struggle with worry because they choose instead to hand their cares to You and trust in Your sufficiency for all they face.

Amen.

Comfort

The Lord has comforted His people,
and will have compassion on His afflicted ones.

ISAIAH 49:13

God of All Comfort,

During times of stress, trial, and sadness throughout my children's lives, I pray that they would know Your Holy Spirit as their Comforter. May Your Spirit bring to my children's minds passages from Your Word about Your sovereignty, Your wisdom, Your power, and how You work in all things for their good. May Your Word help them have the right perspective.

Will You allow them to know Your nearness in everything they face? Thank You that my children can know You as Immanuel—God with us. May this give them strength and courage.

Thank You that even in those difficult times when I can't be there with my children, You will be with them as their Comforter.

Amen.

Spiritual Warfare

*I have given you the authority to trample on snakes
and scorpions and over all the power of the enemy.*

LUKE 10:19

Powerful Conqueror of Hell and the Grave,

Because we are in You, we can be triumphant over the powers of evil. We need not fear Satan and his demons, for their doom is clear in Scripture.

I know that at points along the way, the enemy will come against my children—maybe through some plan to cause them to stumble, maybe by attempting to establish unholy and unhealthy habits in their lives, or maybe in some other dark and sinister way.

May my children resist his attacks and fearlessly stand strong, trusting and obeying You. May the enemy's ploys be crushed and may no stronghold be allowed to form in my children's lives.

Amen.

Courage

The LORD is my light and my salvation—
whom should I fear?
The LORD is the stronghold of my life—
of whom should I be afraid?

PSALM 27:1

Our Strength,

Fear, like a dark shadow, may sometimes fall across my children's hearts. It may arise when they enter an unknown situation, face someone who makes them anxious, or encounter danger.

I ask, Lord, that at each of those times, Your Word and Your promises would come back to the minds of my children. May they recall verses that strengthen them as they consider Your sovereignty, Your power, and Your presence. May the holy light of Your Word push back the shadows from their hearts and minds.

Because of their faith in You, may they find themselves ready to boldly face whatever lies ahead.

Amen.

Obedience

*Everyone who hears these words of Mine
and acts on them will be like a sensible man
who built his house on the rock.*

MATTHEW 7:24

Master,

Even if my children are rich in opportunities to hear Your Word, if they do not act upon it, it is of no benefit to them. I pray that they would be doers of Your Word. May they be wise and love Your instruction.

As they hear Your Word, may they search their own hearts to see what the application should be. May they be tenderhearted and willing to make any necessary changes to their habits and life-styles. May they be quick to accept whatever You are instructing them to do.

When the difficult storms of life come, may my children endure with their faith strong and intact because they trust in You and You alone.

Amen.

Affirmation

There came a voice from heaven:

This is My beloved Son.
I take delight in Him!

MATTHEW 3:17

Our Encourager,

So often, I will speak words of love and affirmation to my children. I pray today, Lord, that through Your Holy Spirit's work, my children will hear these words not just with their ears but in their hearts as well.

May they have an unshakable confidence in how loved and wanted they are. May they always feel my acceptance of them.

It's not a coincidence that Your words in today's passage were spoken before Jesus had actually done anything—before the miracles, before the teaching, before the sacrificial death.

May my children take my words to heart when I tell them that apart from any and all achievements, I love them fully and simply for who they are. Please let this truth take root in their souls and give them great confidence—and may it bear much fruit for Your glory.

Amen.

Honesty

Surely You desire integrity in the inner self.

PSALM 51:6

The One Who Is Truth,

It's not a matter of *if* but *when* children lie. Like all fallen people, at times they will be tempted to avoid the truth, and sometimes they will give in to that temptation. May the training in our home impress upon my children what a detestable thing lying is in the eyes of God.

May my children decide early in their lives that the path of honesty is wisest for them and the one they always wish to follow. May they never get away with even a small lie. Please quickly lead them to confession in these moments.

Would You guide them to so value truthfulness that they would not tolerate even small lies from their closest friends?

Amen.

Missions

The harvest is abundant, but the workers are few.
Therefore, pray to the Lord of the harvest to
send out workers into His harvest.

MATTHEW 9:37-38

Lord of the Harvest,

I pray that my children would have opportunities to hear many missionaries speak of their work. May this make a great and lasting impression on their hearts. As my children grow, may they also read stories of great mission workers.

If You would so bless and allow, may my children have opportunities to participate in short-term mission trips—local, regional, and, if possible, even international. May these greatly mark their hearts with love for all people and a desire for all to know Your good news.

Would You give my children spirits that see their schools, sports teams, and circles of friends as potential mission fields?

Amen.

Worship

LORD, who is like You among the gods?
Who is like You, glorious in holiness,
revered with praises, performing wonders?

EXODUS 15:11

Almighty King of Heaven,

I come today desiring that my children would know You for who You truly are and would respond with reverence. May they have a deep certainty that there is none like You in heaven or on earth. You alone are God.

May their words of praise flow from the love and wonder in their hearts. May they live with a holy awe for You. May their daily actions and the words they speak to others also be acts of worship as they serve You with all they are.

May their great desire be to see You exalted and worshiped for who You are.

Amen.

Appearance

I will praise You
because I have been remarkably and wonderfully made.
Your works are wonderful,
and I know this very well.

PSALM 139:14

Creator,

I come today asking that at some point along the way, my children would not just believe the passage above but would also feel it. May they fully embrace that they are divinely designed by You. May they trust that You made countless detailed choices about them—their body types, hair textures, eye colors, complexions, fingerprints. May they trust that You have skillfully created them and are pleased with Your work.

May knowing that You designed them provide them with strength and confidence in their lives, but may it never lead to pride or arrogance. Please guide them to maintain a healthy balance in this area. May they rightly see themselves as You do.

May their confidence in Your good works and Your acceptance of them be a fortress that keeps them strong when facing issues of self-esteem that plague so many teens and young adults.

Amen.

Testimony

[God] has rescued us from the domain of darkness
and transferred us into the kingdom of the Son He loves.

COLOSSIANS 1:13

Redeemer,

Some people have radical and dramatic stories of coming to faith in You. Others may grow up in Christian homes or hang around people of faith their entire lives, and then one day gently embrace You as their Savior and Lord. However it happens, all praise and honor goes to You!

One day, my children may be called on to tell others about their experiences of receiving You as their Lord and Savior. Regardless of the earthly details of their stories, may they be certain of the spiritual reality that at one point they belonged to the kingdom of darkness, and then they were rescued, redeemed, and brought into Your everlasting Kingdom of light.

I pray that You would use my children's stories for Your glory.

Amen.

Future Spouse

A man who finds a wife finds a good thing
and obtains favor from the LORD.

PROVERBS 18:22

Cornerstone,

Perhaps Your plan for my children includes their remaining single, but if it doesn't, I pray that You would help each of them find the right spouse at the right time. May they have a clear leading from You regarding this relationship, and may You guide them to make a choice not based merely on physical attraction but on true love, commitment, and the conviction that the two of them can serve You better together than they could alone.

Through their relationship together, may they truly know the grace of life found in an intimate union that You have blessed. May they always have You as the center of their relationship and as the foundation they build a life upon together.

Will You guard them from divorce? May there never be even a hint of infidelity, and will You guard them from that temptation? May there never be any abuse but rather a beautiful unity that for decades reflects the evidence that You dwell closely with them.

Prepare both of them even today for what You have for them together in the future.

Amen.

Peace

Peace I leave with you. My peace I give to you.
I do not give to you as the world gives.

JOHN 14:27

Prince of Peace,

This fallen world has always been a place of unrest and turmoil. It will only intensify as we come closer to Your return. Your prophecies are full of unsettling events yet to occur as time runs down for this world.

I pray that my children would know in their hearts a peace that cannot be unseated by any circumstance or event. May they have that constant, abiding peace that comes only from knowing You. May they have a deep and eternally settled sense that all is well between them and their Maker. Give them calm minds and hearts to weather any situation.

May my children have peaceful spirits and sleep well at night because of faith and confidence in You.

Amen.

Teen Rebellion

Rebellion is like the sin of divination,
and defiance is like wickedness and idolatry.

1 SAMUEL 15:23

Most High God,

When it comes to teen rebellion, experience tells us that children will test the limits to see if the consequences will indeed be as they were told. A wise child will learn and submit. A foolish child will persist in doing wrong. This is made clear, Lord, throughout the book of Proverbs.

Rebellion is simply pride fully expressed. It is the immature cry of "I want what I want when I want it." Its twin, stubbornness, will cause children to become arrogant, defiant, and stuck in their places of pride.

God, please grant me wisdom and guide me in identifying early the moments of pride, selfishness, and stubbornness in my children's lives. May You and I together lead my children to have humble, submissive hearts that You will richly bless.

Amen.

Difficulties

In the day of prosperity be joyful,
but in the day of adversity, consider:
God has made the one as well as the other.

ECCLESIASTES 7:14

Lord of All,

Life is filled with such uncertainty. We all have a mix of good days and hard days. There is no way any of us can really predict what lies around the bend for us. The future is in Your hands, and You are sovereign over it all.

I pray that both kinds of days will cause my children to consider the Giver of the day. In the good times, may they always be mindful to express their gratitude to You for even the simple joys.

In the hard times, may Your sovereignty be a comfort to them. May they trust that You have allowed the difficulties for a perfect reason. May they know Your nearness in these times, and even as they endure, may they be at peace.

Amen.

Character of God:
Eternal

From eternity to eternity, You are God.

PSALM 90:2

Eternal King,

You exist outside of time. You are without beginning. You are without end. You have always been and will always be. In this very moment, You exist perfectly in the past, in the present, and in the future. You are never younger and never older—You are truly timeless.

As my children consider this unfathomable truth about You, may it lead them to awe and wonder. Would You make them aware of how brief this mortal life really is and how precious every moment and opportunity we have is?

Would You guide them to worship You in gratitude for the privilege of being with You forever?

Amen.

Teachable Spirit

Instruct a wise man, and he will be wiser still;
teach a righteous man, and he will learn more.

PROVERBS 9:9

Source of All Wisdom,

All truth comes from You. The longing for truth is in the fabric of our souls. Only You can truly satisfy our desire for wisdom.

I pray that my children would have teachable spirits, particularly when it comes to Your Word. May they want to know You in a deeper way.

I pray also about the variety of classroom teachers they will have throughout their lives. May my children be students who are a joy for teachers because of their desire to learn. As instruction and correction come their way, may they welcome them as opportunities to grow and prepare for what You have planned for them in the future.

Amen.

Stewardship of Time

Teach us to number our days carefully
so that we may develop wisdom in our hearts.

PSALM 90:12

Timeless One,

My children cannot yet appreciate, as I do, the brevity of life. But they will learn as they grow that our days truly are a brief morning mist that is here and then gone.

I pray that my children would believe that every day they live is a gift from You and that as the Giver of each day, You know how it can best be spent. May they seek You regarding how to wisely use the precious time they have on this planet.

May they live their days for Your glory, seeing each one as a gift they can give back to You.

Amen.

Self-Control

The fruit of the Spirit is . . . self-control.

GALATIANS 5:22-23

All-Powerful Yet Tender King,

Because You are perfect in all actions and expressions, there is never a need for You to show restraint. Yet because we are fallen, we need Your Spirit to produce within us the fruit of self-control.

I pray that my children would learn to model this with excellence. For Your glory, may they show restraint in their passions and appetites. May they not vent every emotion and thought they think and feel.

May their behavior reflect a wisdom that comes from the presence of Your Holy Spirit.

Amen.

Holiness

How can a young man keep his way pure?
By keeping Your word.

PSALM 119:9

Wonderful Counselor,

Some people seem bent on making every mistake themselves, and they learn lessons that way. Others, the wise ones, look to other people's failures to guide them away from danger and into blessing.

I pray that my children would be among the wise ones who know from a young age that there is no better way to live their lives than to seek Your wisdom for all their steps. May they make time daily to be in Your Word. I pray that they always approach Your Book out of desire rather than duty.

As they learn Your heart and mind, may my children apply Your wisdom to the situations they encounter. May this help them resist sin and experience the blessings of a life characterized by holiness and purity.

I ask that their lives be endless upward spirals of finding that the more they trust You, the more blessed their lives will be, and the more blessed their lives are, the more they will want to trust You.

Amen.

Thought Life

Set your minds on what is above,
not on what is on the earth.

COLOSSIANS 3:2

The Way to Life,

Throughout the day, so many things will scream for my children's attention. Many of these things will be petty and insignificant. I pray that through it all, my children's minds will be like a compass pointing to true north—the Kingdom of Heaven.

I pray that their focus and attention throughout all their days would be on the principles and realities of things above. Though they walk through a world of temporal things, may their eyes and thoughts be on the eternal. May this change everything about their priorities.

Amen.

Parenting: Guidance

Teach a youth about the way he should go;
even when he is old he will not depart from it.

PROVERBS 22:6

Loving Father,

Some things in life I have done Your way. When I did, I was always glad. Some things in life I have done my own way. This has always led to regret. The responsibility of raising children is something I want to do fully Your way.

Help me train my children according to Your wisdom when they are young so they might develop lifelong habits that will bring blessing. Will You be gracious to me and guide me to recall appropriate Scripture verses to use in teachable moments with my children? Please help me seek out and find godly wisdom for this task and not be led by ever-changing worldly thinking.

Will You help me guide my children in ways that are best for their unique designs?

Amen.

Excellence

Whatever you do, do it enthusiastically,
as something done for the Lord and not for men.

COLOSSIANS 3:23

Most Excellent One,

I pray that my children would value excellence in all they do. May they trust that whatever the tasks before them—work around the house, school assignments, projects at their jobs—You have allowed them to come their way. May they desire to reflect Your character in how they work.

May their diligence be a great source of blessing to them.

Will You please guide them to pursue excellence in a healthy, holy way and not in a legalistic, compulsive, unhealthy, or unbalanced manner?

Amen.

Confession

The one who conceals his sins
will not prosper,
but whoever confesses and renounces them
will find mercy.

PROVERBS 28:13

Our Forgiver,

Sometimes when my children are not in my presence, they will face temptation. Because You are the Redeemer, You can even use their failures to help them learn how to stand strong the next time they face the same sin.

Sometimes when my children sin, no one besides You and them knows about it. I pray in those moments that, because of Your Spirit's prompting, my children will be quick to confess their sins and seek forgiveness. May they not continue to conceal their failures. May their hearts be tender and obedient to Your earliest call to confession.

May the sweetness of the mercy and grace they will surely find with You lead them to always be prompt in confessing their sins.

Amen.

Protection

I will seek refuge in the shadow of Your wings
until danger passes.

PSALM 57:1

Our Refuge,

We see a picture of You as a caring parent in today's verse. What a comfort it is that this is Your heart for Your children.

There will be times when I can't be there to provide shelter and protection for my children. I pray they will learn early the wisdom of calling out to You in these moments. May they run to You and find that You are a faithful refuge for them. May they find that You physically protect them, and may their spirits find that when they move near to Your side, there is always calm and peace.

Amen.

Evangelism

Follow Me . . . and I will make you fish for people!

MATTHEW 4:19

Savior,

I pray often that my children would be so captivated and consumed by Your beautiful gospel that it is ever on their minds. May
they live with awe and wonder that in Your great mercy You have
redeemed them.

May this amazement lead them to want others to know the gift of
salvation You offer. May it be their heartbeat to see others rescued
from the kingdom of darkness and brought into Your Kingdom of
light.

May they speak boldly and unashamedly about believing that
You are the Way, the Truth, and the Life and that no one comes to
the Father except through You. Would You lead them to know the
incredible blessing of seeing those with whom they share the gospel
come to faith?

Amen.

Bullies

Deliver me, my God, from the power of the wicked,
from the grasp of the unjust and oppressive.

PSALM 71:4

Our Defender,

At some point, hopefully later than sooner, my children will have to deal with peers who will try to intimidate, bully, or take advantage of them. I pray even now that You would prepare my children for that moment.

May they be secure in knowing Your hand is on their lives and that You can take care of them and lead them through the situation. May they be able to look beyond the immediate tension and emotion of the moment and consider the heart and soul of the one oppressing them.

May they cry out to You in that time for Your deliverance. Will Your Spirit's nearness calm their fear, give them words of wisdom, and protect them?

May they even pray for the salvation of the one offending them. If You allow them the opportunity, may my children express forgiveness to that person.

Amen.

Speech

Praising and cursing come out of the same mouth.
My brothers, these things should not be this way.
Does a spring pour out sweet and bitter water from
the same opening? Can a fig tree produce olives,
my brothers, or a grapevine produce figs? Neither
can a saltwater spring yield fresh water.

JAMES 3:10-12

Lover of Pure Speech,

I pray that as my children grow, especially as teenagers and into young adulthood, there will be godly consistency in their language. May they not speak one way at home and another, coarser way with their friends.

May the punch and power of profanity never hold an attraction for them or the friends they choose to be around. May their every-day words consistently reflect the language they use to lift You up in worship and devotion.

Amen.

Spiritual Gifts

According to the grace given to us,
we have different gifts.

ROMANS 12:6

Creator,

Not only have You amazingly created us physically; You have formed each of us with unique combinations of spiritual gifts. The varieties and combinations of giftings are mind-blowing. You have formed each of us with great purpose regarding how we can serve You. As we serve You with our gifts and abilities, it will mean glory for You and joy for us.

I can't yet imagine all You have placed within my children, but I live with great anticipation that their giftings will be revealed in time. All types of spiritual gifts are exciting—wisdom, knowledge, faith, service, encouragement, giving, mercy, helping others in need, and leadership.

I don't have specific dreams for what I would like my children's vocations and/or ministries to look like; I simply want my kids to seek after Your leading and discover how You have uniquely wired them. Will You guide them on the journey of discovering their gifts and their places of service?

Amen.

Control

Don't get drunk with wine, which leads to reckless actions, but be filled by the Spirit.

EPHESIANS 5:18

Lord,

The best of life is always found when all we are is submitted to Your control. When Your Holy Spirit fills and directs a believer, the outcome will ultimately be joy, peace, hope, and untold good things.

I pray that my children would not give over control of themselves, even for brief periods of time, to anything or anyone besides You. A number of substances, legal and illegal, may tempt them along the way, but in those moments, may they see the value and holy wisdom in not allowing themselves to be mastered by anything other than You.

Please guide them with the strength to stand strong and resist temptation. May they choose instead to hold to the freedom You give.

Amen.

Goodness

As we have opportunity,
we must work for the good of all,
especially for those who belong
to the household of faith.

GALATIANS 6:10

Good Shepherd,

In a world where people are so used to seeing others behave in ways that are unkind and self-serving, You have called us to be a different and special people. It will seem strange and fascinating to the world to watch people who actively seek opportunities to do good to others.

I pray that my children would be among those people the world will see always speaking and showing kindness and love to others.

May this simply be the fruitful overflow of Your love and goodness within them.

Amen.

Excellence

Be diligent to present yourself approved to God,
a worker who doesn't need to be ashamed,
correctly teaching the word of truth.

2 TIMOTHY 2:15

Most Excellent God,

I ask today that You would put within my children's hearts the desire to pursue excellence in all their endeavors. May they never be accused of being lazy, and may they wisely choose the things in which they will invest their efforts and energy.

Would You guide them to be self-motivated and driven in a healthy way? May this determination show in their schoolwork and their employment. May they be zealous about doing quality work.

May this come from their desire to reflect Your excellence in all things

Amen.

Negative Influences

How happy is the man
who does not follow the advice of the wicked
or take the path of sinners
or join a group of mockers!

PSALM 1:1

Deliverer,

As my children's world expands, there will more and more acquaintances that as a parent I might consider bad influences. Some of these will be what Your Word would call fools. I ask that in those moments of first encounter, Your Spirit would be active in my children's hearts.

The wisest thing for them would be to not engage with the unwise. May they certainly not linger in these relationships.

May they sense Your Spirit's leading and heed Your voice telling them to simply walk away.

Amen.

Purity

*To the pure, everything is pure, but to those
who are defiled and unbelieving nothing is pure;
in fact, both their mind and conscience are defiled.*

TITUS 1:15

Holy King of Heaven,

I pray today asking that my children would be pure minded.
May they retain a childlikeness and innocence about them.

There will be times when they hear off-color jokes, sexual references, and innuendos and not comprehend the meaning. May they
have peace in those moments, knowing that to pursue the meaning would simply lead them down shadowed hallways into darker
places. May they be content simply to let the moment of curiosity
pass them by.

May they be pure in heart, always believing the best of others
and seeking Your honor in all situations. Will You continue to refine
them so that all sin and worldly affections may be confessed? May
the focus of their hearts and minds be singularly set on Your glory.

Amen.

Contentment

We brought nothing into the world,
and we can take nothing out.
But if we have food and clothing,
we will be content with these.

1 TIMOTHY 6:7-8

Satisfier of Our Souls,

I know at some point along the way, the clawing fingers of money, consumerism, and possessions will strive to place their grip around my children's hearts. I pray this will always only be a temporary state that is quickly ended. May my children have great faith in You as the Provider of their daily bread and clothing. May they choose to value and pursue treasures that are eternal and not the temporary ones that nature and time destroy.

May my children find their riches in their relationships with You and with others. May they clearly know how to discern between their wants and needs, and may they choose wisely and accordingly.

Amen.

Pride

Before his downfall a man's heart is proud,
but humility comes before honor.

PROVERBS 18:12

Excellent One,

I pray that my children will have right perspectives. May they always see You as first and foremost in importance. May they also be mindful to consider others as more important than themselves.

Would You guard them from slipping into the shadow lands of pride? Would You guide them to be so content with Your sufficiency and Your love for them that they won't feel the need to exalt themselves? Would You help them be aware of pride when they see it expressed in others and to be so turned off by it that they want to ensure that it never takes root in their own hearts?

May there be many times when the humble, quiet, excellent way my children go about their work causes others to recognize them and honor them for what they do.

Amen.

Forgiveness

If we confess our sins,
[God] is faithful and righteous
to forgive us our sins and to cleanse us
from all unrighteousness.

1 JOHN 1:9

Faithful Forgiver,

I don't live under any illusion that my children will live perfect lives. I know they will make mistakes, fail, and even have moments of rebellion against what is right. I ask that these moments would not be the pattern of their lives, and may the episodes be few and far between.

When my children sin, Lord, I pray they would be quick to ask for forgiveness. May they be tender and sensitive to Your Spirit's voice of conviction.

In their moments of confession, I ask that today's passage would be a jewel they treasure and return to often. May it give them confidence and peace because of the certainty of Your grace and cleansing.

Amen.

Competition

*If anyone competes as an athlete, he is not crowned
unless he competes according to the rules.*

2 TIMOTHY 2:5

Righteous Judge,

I pray that my children would have a competitive streak.
However, may they allow this part of their personalities to be under
your lordship, and may it show itself in ways that are good and holy.

I do pray that in sporting activities, school studies, and artistic ventures, my children would strive for excellence and victory.
May they model determination and perseverance. May they also be
committed to fairness.

I pray that in their spiritual lives, they would strive with zeal
and great discipline to be victorious over their own flesh and selfish desires. May they pursue the prize of knowing and experiencing
You more.

Amen.

God's Word

How I love Your instruction!
It is my meditation all day long.

PSALM 119:97

Heavenly Father,

I pray that I would teach my children to deeply love Your Word by example and not just through instruction. I know they will observe so many moments in my life when I don't think they are looking. May they "catch" me going to Your Word on many occasions.

May they see in me a reverence, desire, and love for Scripture. May they see Your Word bear fruit in my life such that they desire it for their own lives.

May it be that they would see and understand in my example, more than in my words, why they should love Your Word.

Bless You for Your perfect and holy Word. May it shine brightly from my life into the lives of my children.

Amen.

Family Time

How happy is everyone who fears the LORD,
who walks in His ways! . . .
Your wife will be like a fruitful vine
within your house,
your sons, like young olive trees
around your table.

PSALM 128:1, 3

Great Provider,

May our meals together be sweet times of family togetherness. I know how important it is to take time out of a busy day to sit together and remember Your provision, and I am thankful for the opportunity to hear about everyone's day. Often in times like these, I am given a window into the hearts of my children.

I pray that You would grant me wisdom to read these moments well as we eat and talk. Help me know when to properly instruct, comfort, encourage, and dream with my children—whatever is needed in the moment. I invite You to dwell closely with us in these times. May You be honored through our love, conversation, and laughter together.

Amen.

Submission to Authority

Everyone must submit to the governing authorities,
for there is no authority except from God, and
those that exist are instituted by God.

ROMANS 13:1

God of Order,

You have established the idea of authority and submission. We see it in the Trinity. We see it in the church. We see it in families. We see it in work relations.

I pray that my children will take You at Your Word, trust You, and willingly submit to all levels of leadership, if that leadership is aligned with Your Word. I pray that in their classrooms, on athletic teams, and in places of employment, my children would be among those who willingly submit to authority and cannot be swayed into rebellion.

Amen.

Priorities

Love the Lord your God with all your heart,
with all your soul, with all your mind,
and with all your strength.

MARK 12:30

Our Loving Father,

You know how passionately and persistently I pray that my children will have a right relationship with You. Of all the words that might describe that relationship, may the one that looms largest be *love*.

As Your Word calls them to, may they love You with every part of who they are—with all their being, with all their emotion and passion, with all their thoughts and intellect, and with all their physical capabilities. May their love never be empty words or empty ritual but instead always be living and active.

Please guide their lives such that loving You is a priority to them.

Amen.

Joy

The fruit of the Spirit is . . . joy.

GALATIANS 5:22

Giver of Joy,

To know You, Father, is to know joy. I pray that throughout their lives, my children would know that deep-down sense of well-being that comes when all is right between them and their Maker.

May this overflow of knowing You produce real hope and peace. May it remain strong and unaffected by circumstances or anything that anyone else might do or say to them.

Your Son, Jesus, was able to endure the worst of earthly moments for the joy of the relationship He had with You, the Father. May my children endure the hard times they face and never lose the joy of simply belonging to You.

Amen.

Compassion

Rejoice with those who rejoice;
weep with those who weep.

ROMANS 12:15

Perfect One,

You have so graciously filled Your people with Your Spirit, giving us the ability to act in ways that are not the norm but are actually supernatural. In our flesh, we might be resentful of the successes of others and delight in their hardships; but because of Your Spirit, we can move toward them with compassion and join with them in what they are experiencing in life.

I pray that my children would be so trusting of Your good hand in their lives that they are free to share joy with others who are experiencing blessings and honor.

May my children also be moved to show kindness and compassion toward others in difficult situations. Would You help them, in love, shed tears with others facing times of disappointment, hardship, or sorrow?

Amen.

Physical Health

Don't you know that your body
is a sanctuary of the Holy Spirit?

1 CORINTHIANS 6:19

Creator,

I pray that my children would be mindful of being stewards of the physical bodies You have given them. Because their bodies, along with all they have, belong to You, they are Yours to use. May my children excel in the care and stewardship of the body.

May they have the strength to fight bad impulses in their food choices. May they stay away from junk food, or at least use good discretion and moderation in making decisions about it. May they avoid opportunities to indulge in harmful and addictive substances.

I pray that my children would adopt healthy lifestyles, including good nutrition, exercise, and adequate sleep. May they present their bodies to You as living sacrifices for Your glory.

Amen.

Complaining

Do not grumble.

1 CORINTHIANS 10:10, NIV

God of All Provision,

Throughout history, Your people have tasted richly of Your physical and spiritual provision yet allowed self-centeredness and grumbling to control their lives. I ask that this would never be true of my children.

Would You guide them to trust in Your love, Your will, and Your provision for them so that even during the leaner seasons of life, they would not complain? Would You guide them to trust that You have chosen the ones who are in positions of authority over them, and would You help them willingly, even joyfully, submit?

May You weed out any self-centeredness in their hearts so that they will never grumble or express discontentment toward You. Please guide them to have contented, peaceful, patient, and trusting hearts.

Amen.

Character of God: Sovereign

The Most High . . .
does what He wants with the army of heaven
and the inhabitants of the earth.

DANIEL 4:34-35

Most High God,

You are sovereign. You reign from the throne of heaven. Throughout all creation, You do what pleases You; and whatever You do, You do with perfection. There is no throne higher than Yours; no power in heaven, in hell, or on earth can thwart Your plans. All people, creatures, and objects do Your bidding.

As my children come to learn this truth about You, I pray it would bring them enduring comfort. May they trust that You oversee their lives and that anything that comes against them (trials, afflictions, problems) has already passed through Your hand, and You are allowing it for a reason. May it give them peace that not one moment of their lives is without a plan and purpose.

May they find great rest in Your sovereignty.

Amen.

Responsibility

Whoever is faithful in very little
is also faithful in much,
and whoever is unrighteous in very little
is also unrighteous in much.

LUKE 16:10

Master,

Bless You, Lord, that You love us enough to deal with each of us individually. You give us all unique and differing talents and responsibilities and hold us accountable for what we do with them.

I pray that as my children are given new responsibilities from You, they would never resent a task they feel is beneath their abilities. May they instead trust that You are working perfectly, and therefore the wisest choice for them is to be excellent in the work before them. May my children prove their faithfulness by being responsible for the little that is theirs to do.

May this hold true not just in how they handle talents but also in how they handle their finances. Would You bless their faithfulness with a greater capacity for service here on earth, as well as one day in Your heavenly Kingdom?

Amen.

Presence of God

As for me, God's presence is my good.

PSALM 73:28

The One Who Loves Us,

I pray today that my children would always have a desire to draw near to You. May they find that, even from a young age, when time is spent in Your presence, hope is renewed, trust is strengthened, and perspective is gained.

May my children greatly desire times of corporate gathering to worship You. Please help them come to love time alone in Your Word, hearing Your heart and sitting at Your feet.

May their longing for intimacy with You be a flame in their souls that grows stronger through each passing year of their lives.

Amen.

Idolatry

Flee from idolatry.

1 CORINTHIANS 10:14

One True God,

We are a people who have been made to worship. There are longings deep within us—desires for love, beauty, purpose, significance, acceptance—that are meant to lead us to You. These desires are truly satisfied only when we have our whole focus fixed on You. Yet many people look to other things to satisfy these longings.

While I don't fear that my children will bow down and worship figures of wood or stone, other idols will strive to get a grip on their hearts.

God, will You guard and protect them from ever trying to find deep meaning and satisfaction in the idols of this world, such as power, popularity, status, achievement, success, money, appearance, and approval? These are all insidious vines that strive to capture our hearts. Please give my children the strength to reject them as sources of true meaning and hope.

May they continually choose to love only You as the One who is on the throne of their lives.

Amen.

Adventure of Faith

You are my rock and my fortress;
You lead and guide me
because of Your name.

PSALM 31:3

God Who Leads,

I pray that my children would experience the adventure of faith, where Your calling is clear, the task is great, and their own power and wisdom are not sufficient for the work at hand. If something is going to be done, You will have to accomplish it. Yet You invite them to join You in achieving great things.

Though they may feel overwhelmed by the challenges before them, may they trust You. May they not play it safe. May they embrace risk, stepping out beyond their comfort zones, deeply aware of their constant need of and dependence on You.

As a result, may they know You and Your faithfulness as they would never know You otherwise.

Amen.

Witness

You are the salt of the earth. . . .
You are the light of the world.

MATTHEW 5:13-14

Savior,

Because we've been forever changed by Your grace, we will stand out as being different from the people of this world. I pray that just as salt in biblical times was used primarily as a preservative, my children's righteousness would help slow the decay of this present world. I pray that their lives would be a seasoning that leads people of the world to thirst for the hope my children have found in You.

I pray also that their lives would shine as godly examples of Your great power. May their words and actions testify to Your grace and mercy. May my children never be afraid or ashamed to be known as Yours, but may their good deeds burn brightly and boldly before a watching world.

Amen.

Critical Spirit

Why do you look at the speck in your brother's eye
but don't notice the log in your own eye?

MATTHEW 7:3

Perfect Judge,

I pray that You would guard my children from having critical spirits. May they never develop a spirit of pride where they look down on others and feel self-satisfied or superior. May they never feel that it is their place to pass judgment on others.

May they instead be so aware of their own shortcomings and the goodness of Your grace that has been extended to them that they maintain gentle, humble spirits.

May they indeed try to help others who are struggling with failures in their lives, but may they do it from a place of love and tender care.

Amen.

Peacemaking

Make every effort to keep the unity of
the Spirit through the bond of peace.

EPHESIANS 4:3, NIV

One Who Speaks Peace,

Though we live in a world where the natural thing to do is to be selfish and demand our own way, that choice will always result in tension and a lack of unity. I pray that my children would instead pursue the pattern of Your Kingdom.

Would You guide my children to seek to maintain peace in relationships? May they have a gentle humility that gives them great patience in dealing with others. Would You guide them not to be easily angered but to always be quick to forgive?

Amen.

Laziness

Don't love sleep, or you will become poor;
open your eyes, and you'll have enough to eat.

PROVERBS 20:13

Our Fervent God,

You have given us work to do that will give our lives meaning. By being diligent and striving for excellence, we can reflect Your character to the world and bring You glory.

I pray that my children would never be lazy but would be intentional and seek to excel at whatever work is before them. May they please You with an industrious spirit and a good work ethic. May they bring joy to those who have given them assignments to do.

May my children always be blessed with the good reward that comes to those who work hard and provide well for their families. May they never know the lack of respect that comes to those who are lazy and unmotivated.

Amen.

Beauty

*Your beauty should not consist of outward things like
elaborate hairstyles and the wearing of gold ornaments
or fine clothes. Instead, it should consist of what is inside
the heart with the imperishable quality of a gentle and
quiet spirit, which is very valuable in God's eyes.*

1 PETER 3:3-4

Creator,

Even from a young age, my children will encounter thousands of messages telling them what constitutes beauty for women. As they struggle with defining *beauty*, I pray that my children would whole-heartedly trust the truth of Your Word speaking to them.

This will go against the grain of the culture, but will You lead them to value the beauty of a woman's quiet, gentle spirit far above any look that can be gained through makeup and fleeting fashion trends? May they believe that spiritual virtue is always more important than external appearance.

May my children value what is imperishable over what is temporary and fading.

Amen.

Money

The love of money is a root of all kinds of evil,
and by craving it, some have wandered away from the
faith and pierced themselves with many pains.

1 TIMOTHY 6:10

God Who Is Our Inheritance,

I want my children to always pursue higher things. I want their hearts to be set on the Kingdom above and not on the temporary kingdom of this world.

May they realize that they are simply stewards of all You entrust to them. If You choose them to steward a great amount of earthly riches, that's wonderful, but may they never develop a love for money.

May they always wisely discern the difference between their wants and their needs. And may they live like all their wealth, not just a portion, belongs to You.

Amen.

Faith

If you have faith the size of a mustard seed,
you will tell this mountain, "Move from here to there,"
and it will move. Nothing will be impossible for you.

MATTHEW 17:20

The One Who Is Worthy of Our Faith,

I ask that You give my children faith that is always active, growing, and maturing. As new circumstances and situations come along, I pray they would trust You as You lead them. May they have full confidence that spiritual things are just as real as the things their eyes can see.

I pray that they would be so sure of Your existence, Your holiness, Your glory, Your love, and Your nearness that this certainty would be a guiding principle for all their decisions. May they have courage to take chances and brave steps of faith to follow Your lead. May it give them great strength and confidence that if any venture, plan, or dream is in accordance with Your will, nothing will be impossible.

Amen.

God's Word

*I have treasured Your word in my heart
so that I may not sin against You.*

PSALM 119:11

Word of God,

I come today asking that You might give my children a love for memorizing Your Word. If that skill does not come easy for them, would You let them see the benefit of it and give them a desire to do the hard work anyway?

I pray that they would commit to memory Scripture verses that will help them recognize the approach of the enemy early. May these verses also direct them as to how they can live holy lives that are pleasing to You and easy for You to bless.

It's not enough for them simply to know Your Word and recognize sin; may they also apply Your truth to every area and relationship of their lives and be doers of Your Word.

Amen.

Spiritual Leaders

Now we ask you, brothers, to give recognition
to those who labor among you and lead you in
the Lord and admonish you, and to regard them
very highly in love because of their work.

1 THESSALONIANS 5:12-13

Great Shepherd,

Today I come to lift up our church pastors and other ministers—particularly their relationships with my children. May they truly be leaders of integrity who intimately hear You speak truth into their lives. May they passionately love and obey You.

From that overflow, may their ministries be valued by my children. From the pulpit, may these leaders help ground my children in the truth of Your Word. In personal interactions, may their care and concern be meaningful to my children.

While I pray for our pastors, I also want to be mindful of other teachers and leaders at our church. May my children's time with them be fruitful and bring about growth in their lives. May our family always have an attitude of respect, appreciation, and honor for our spiritual leaders.

Amen.

Diligence

Whatever your hands find to do,
do with all your strength.

ECCLESIASTES 9:10

Master,

At some point in life, my children will find themselves caught in a transitional or waiting season. They may find themselves in a class or school program they don't wish to be in, or in a job that isn't quite what they were hoping for. Whenever this happens, may they still pursue excellence in whatever they do.

Would You help them maintain hope, trusting that You fully see where they are and that You have allowed them to be there in these times of waiting? May they commit themselves to doing the best they can with what is before them every moment. Though it may be work they feel is not a good fit for them, or may even be beneath their abilities, may they take it on with a passion for excellence.

Amen.

Assurance

I am persuaded that not even death or life,
angels or rulers,
things present or things to come, hostile powers,
height or depth, or any other created thing
will have the power to separate us
from the love of God that is in Christ Jesus our Lord!

ROMANS 8:38-39

Unchanging One,

I come before You today asking that my children wouldn't wrestle with doubts about whether You love them. May they always see Your cross as the final word declaring just how totally, fully, and eternally they are loved.

May today's verse be of great comfort and assurance to them. Though they may face hardships, trouble, danger, temptation, persecution, and even death for You, may they never wonder if they are securely held in Your love. Though their love for You may at times falter, may they live never questioning whether something will separate them from Your great love.

Amen.

Uniqueness

My bones were not hidden from You
when I was made in secret,
when I was formed in the depths of the earth.
Your eyes saw me when I was formless;
all my days were written in Your book and planned
before a single one of them began.

PSALM 139:15-16

One and Only God,

There are no others You have formed in all of history who are exactly like my children. Bless You, God of inexhaustible creativity!

In a world where there is immense pressure to conform, would You set my children's hearts at peace with being who they uniquely are? May this be a strength that allows them to pursue their individual passions and dreams. May they be victorious over the temptations to compare themselves with others.

Would You give my children courage to pursue the paths in life You uniquely offer to them? May they find it a joy and an adventure to be one of a kind.

Amen.

Prayer

*Pray at all times in the Spirit
with every prayer and request.*

EPHESIANS 6:18

God Who Hears Our Hearts,

My children will often hear my voice in prayer—offering blessings for meals, lifting up concerns for our family, interceding for friends.

Through those prayers, Lord, please let my children hear my heart. May I be mindful to give voice to prayers that focus on my devotion to You.

May I speak of my trust in You. May I express words of praise and adoration of You. Please guide me to speak aloud words of confession and repentance.

May my children not just hear my *words* but actually witness my *heart* as I come before Your throne.

Amen.

Physical Health

Please test your servants for 10 days. Let us
be given vegetables to eat and water to drink. Then
examine our appearance and the appearance of the
young men who are eating the king's food.

DANIEL 1:12-13

Way of Life,

I know that my children, like many others, might be attracted to brightly packaged, highly advertised, and nutritionally empty foods. I pray that they would exercise great wisdom in making food and beverage choices.

May they be drawn to good, healthy meats and grains, vegetables and fruits, and water as a beverage of choice. Would You guide them to enjoy making wise decisions, as well as enjoying the results of those choices?

I know they will be tempted by lesser choices, but would You lead them to practice self-control and moderation? Would You help them not develop poor habits? And please keep them from struggling with eating disorders.

May they enjoy blessing You for the excellent foods You provide for us.

Amen.

Compassion

The Lord is very compassionate and merciful.

JAMES 5:11

Our Tenderhearted Savior,

You were moved with mercy by our fallen condition, and You took action. I pray that my children would emulate You in this way.

May their eyes see the need in the world around them. May their hearts be moved with compassion for the outcast, unwanted, unloved, neglected, orphaned, aged, addicted, and homeless. Would You guide them to give their time as well as their resources to showing kindness and mercy and offering relief to those in need?

Please help me set a good example for my children by modeling a life of charity and compassion.

Amen.

Love

Let no one despise your youth; instead, you should
be an example to the believers in . . . love.

1 TIMOTHY 4:12

Lord of Love,

Your idea of love is radically different from the emotion our culture calls love. Your Word helps us see that real love is self-sacrificing service on behalf of others, regardless of our feelings or emotions.

I pray that my children would be wildly different from this world in the way they love. May their example be a beautiful display of Your humble service and how You continually care more about others than about Yourself.

May their lives be winsome and compelling in the way they emulate Your love.

Amen.

Obedience

This is what love for God is:
to keep His commands.

1 JOHN 5:3

Lord of Truth and Wisdom,

The evidence of real faith is love—love for You, love for Your people, love for Your Word.

The evidence of love for You is a desire to obey Your Word. I pray this desire will be strong and real in the hearts of my children.

May it be, Lord, that my children so delight in Your Word that obedience is a joyful expression of their love for You. May their obedience never come from a legalistic, grudging compliance but from a deep inner trust in Your wisdom and belief in the blessings that come to those who obey.

Amen.

Sharing

Do what is good . . . be rich in good works . . .
be generous, willing to share.

1 TIMOTHY 6:18

Our Generous God,

Whether or not my children ever have a lot of money to steward, they will have rich blessings because of Your presence in their lives. I pray they would be unselfish. Would You lead them to always care deeply about the needs of others and to be generous in responding to those needs?

Whatever they have, may they be willing to share with others. Even from a young age, may my children freely share whatever they have with siblings and friends.

Though some will take advantage of their generosity, may this not deter my children from trusting You with all that You entrust to them.

Amen.

Speech

*If anyone thinks he is religious without
controlling his tongue, then his religion is
useless and he deceives himself.*

JAMES 1:26

Holy One,

My children's words will often be the clearest window into what's going on in their souls. I pray that the overflow of their lips would testify that their souls are right with You.

Would You convict my children of any lying, angry or impure speech, and slanderous words? May they instead, by their words, be shining examples of self-control. May they choose to speak what brings life, hope, and healing, and may their words demonstrate the authenticity of their faith.

May blessings come to them because of the truthfulness of their words.

Amen.

Encouragement

*Let us be concerned about one another in order
to promote love and good works.*

HEBREWS 10:24

Our Great Hope,

We all need brothers and sisters to draw near to us as we walk this road of faith. Seeing the faith of others encourages us to stay strong.

I pray that my children would always have dear members of the household of faith to walk close beside them. May their example and influence guide my children into lives of greater fruitfulness.

I also ask that my children would in turn have the same good influence on many other people. May they recognize the potential in others and help fan their gifts and talents into full flame. May my children's words encourage others to grow in faith and journey on with hope and strength.

Amen.

Hope

*Always be ready to give a defense to anyone who
asks you for a reason for the hope that is in you.*

1 PETER 3:15

Hope of the Nations,

I pray that my children's lives would radiate with the hope they
have in You. May they be so obviously out of step with the dominant
culture that it would cause others to wonder why.

Whenever people ask about their faith, whether in formal or
informal settings, may they be prepared to give answers with great
clarity and conviction. Would You meet them in those moments?
May they respond in tones of humility, gentleness, and care for
others while displaying a great reverence and regard for You.

May the hope within them be a shining light that draws others
to who You are.

Amen.

Protection

I will be with you
when you pass through the waters,
and when you pass through the rivers,
they will not overwhelm you.
You will not be scorched
when you walk through the fire,
and the flame will not burn you.

ISAIAH 43:2

Our Fortress,

The home You have designed for us in Your Kingdom will be a safe place. But this fallen world is not safe. I care about many things in my life, but nothing compares to how much I care for my children. When I think about the big, frightening world they must face, I am tempted to worry. However, I will choose to trust You and continue praying for Your care and protection over my children.

When they face physical dangers, keep them safe. In trials and temptations, hold them close. When they encounter peer pressure, strengthen them and keep them from crumbling. When suffering seems overwhelming, may they find rest and refuge in You.

Will You take all things the enemy intends for harm in my children's lives and use them for good? They are my precious children, God, and I entrust them to Your care.

Amen.

Grudges

Whenever you stand praying,
if you have anything against anyone, forgive him,
so that your Father in heaven will also
forgive you your wrongdoing.

MARK 11:25

Our Faithful Forgiver,

I pray that my children would learn to develop times of prayer as sweet communion with You. May they come before You with open hearts, willing to hear You speak to them about any sins or compromises in their lives.

As they are before You, Lord, should You bring to mind someone with whom my children have an unreconciled relationship, may they be quick to do whatever it takes to make things right. May my children not hold on to bitterness or anger toward others. May unforgiveness never linger within their hearts, and may they always show grace at the first opportunity.

Amen.

Pressure

We were under great pressure,
far beyond our ability to endure. . . .
But this happened that we might not
rely on ourselves but on God.

2 CORINTHIANS 1:8-9, NIV

Lord in Whose Presence Is Peace,

I've never known a time when kids faced the kinds of pressures they do now. They are pressured to not just do well academically but to consistently excel. They are pressured to be outstanding in every possible pursuit.

God, You know that I want my children to do well in their pursuits and to apply themselves, but please keep me from driving them in unhealthy ways. Reveal to me if this is something I do but am unaware of. I want my children to dream and reach and strive, but only in ways that are life-giving and balanced, not in ways where their self-worth and value depend on their success. I want them to enjoy their school years and not resent them.

Help my children rely on Your strength in the midst of pressure. May they find their identity in You, not in performance or achievement.

Amen.

Trust

Trust in the LORD and do what is good;
dwell in the land and live securely.

PSALM 37:3

Lord,

I pray that Your name would be written on the hearts of my children. May they be sure of who You are. May they have great confidence that You reign over all things and are worthy of their trust and obedience. May they give You all of themselves.

Out of that confidence, may they live lives that are rich and overflowing with good deeds. May their hearts be loving and kind toward everyone they encounter.

Because they live to be a blessing to others, may Your rich blessings fall across every area of their lives.

Amen.

Character of God: All-Powerful

Now to Him who is able to do
above and beyond all that we ask or think
according to the power that works in us.

EPHESIANS 3:20

All-Powerful One,

You are perfect in power. The power You had in the past and will have in the future will never be more, or less, than the power You have now. All power is Yours. Your power gave us creation. Your power preserves and holds all things together. Your power accomplished salvation, and in power You will one day judge all people.

May my children trust in You as the almighty One, and may their confidence in who You are give them great peace and hope. May they at times tremble before You in holy reverence—awed by Your greatness.

May it be a great comfort to them that nothing is too hard for You. There is no prayer You cannot answer, no need You cannot meet, and no temptation You cannot give my children strength to overcome.

Amen.

Mercy

Be merciful,
just as your Father also is merciful.

LUKE 6:36

Merciful Savior,

You withhold from us the punishment we deserve. You provide a way when we are helpless. You lavish Your mercy upon us. Your grace and forgiveness are never-ending.

I pray that just as Your heart was moved, may my children's hearts be moved by those who are in need. Would You lead them not just to feel compassion but also to take action and bring aid? For those in physical need, may my children take wise and helpful steps to lend a hand to the poor, the outcast, the orphaned, and those in distress.

More importantly, for those in spiritual need, may my children speak words of hope, encouragement, and truth that will be merciful and life-giving as they share Your good news.

Amen.

Abundant Life

*I have come so that they may have life
and have it in abundance.*

JOHN 10:10

Life Giver,

Life with You is the deepest, richest experience anyone could hope for in the here and now and beyond. I desire this depth of blessing for my children.

With You as their Savior, may they drink deeply of the spiritual riches that are theirs through Your grace—eternal life in Your blessed presence.

May they experience the abundant life You offer during their earthly days. May they know Your comfort, peace, hope, joy, strength, and love even this very day.

Amen.

Solitude

[Jesus] often withdrew to deserted places and prayed.

LUKE 5:16

Father Who Draws Near,

Just as Your Son did during His earthly ministry, I pray that my children would be intentional in finding times of solitude. I ask that my children would never fear being alone but rather would enjoy it. I'm not asking that they would be loners—I want them to delight in being with people—but I'm asking that You would guide them to find a healthy, holy balance.

Will You teach my children how to use their time well when they are alone? As young children, may they know how to entertain themselves. As they grow, will You help them value purity? May they guard their minds, their lips, their ears, and what they set before their eyes when they are alone.

May they use times of solitude to draw near to You, seek You, and find strength for what You have ahead for them.

Amen.

Growing Spiritually

Jesus increased . . . in favor with God.

LUKE 2:52

Giver and Builder of Our Faith,

I pray that You would use our home and the years my children will spend here to build in them a strong faith. May they encounter challenges along the way that compel them to trust You. May they experience for themselves how faithful, kind, and good You are.

May they be diligent about being in Your Word and praying throughout the day. May they have opportunities to share what they are learning about You with other believers, as well as chances to share Your good news with those who don't know You yet.

May their faith be active—always growing, always risking, always trusting.

Amen.

Purity

Your eyes are too pure to look on evil,
and You cannot tolerate wrongdoing.

HABAKKUK 1:13

Heaven's Holy One,

This world will assault my children's eyes with immorality. The opportunities to look upon impure and sinful things will be limitless. I pray that even when they are young, we would be able to talk about this.

Would You help them believe in the value of purity? Though in their flesh they will want to look at things they should not, would You guide them to embrace the greater treasure of holiness?

May they develop early the defenses they will need to handle the countless moments when they encounter temptation. Would You guide my children to experience success in looking to You and not to the sinful things of this world?

Amen.

Leadership

*Whoever wants to become great among you
must be your servant, and whoever wants to
be first among you must be a slave to all.*

MARK 10:43-44

Our Great Servant-Leader,

I pray that because of the strength of my children's faith and convictions, and because of Your calling on their lives, they would have the confidence to lead others. I also ask that You guide them to model their leadership styles after Yours.

May my children view leadership roles as opportunities to serve—always showing others love, hope, and encouragement. I ask that this posture would grow from humble hearts and that they would never consider themselves superior.

May their lives show that they view others as more important than themselves, and may my children have a deep sense of care and compassion, demonstrating lives of devotion to others.

Amen.

Humor

All the days of the oppressed are miserable,
but a cheerful heart has a continual feast.

PROVERBS 15:15

God of Joy,

The sound of a child laughing is beautiful music to the heart of any parent. Father, You desire for Your children to know deep joy, and I want the same for mine.

May my children be quick to laugh, but not at the expense of others, and not at things that are coarse, crude, or worldly. May they recognize the humor in daily situations, and may they experience often how laughter can create a bridge to new or deeper friendships.

May they also not take themselves too seriously but be the first to laugh at their own foibles in healthy, holy ways.

Amen.

Discipline

The one who follows instruction is on the path to life,
but the one who rejects correction goes astray.

PROVERBS 10:17

Giver of Wisdom from on High,

No discipline seems pleasant at the time, whether it comes from a parent, a teacher, or You, our heavenly Father. In times of discipline, may my children know the heart of the One who is leading them and trust that Your discipline is always for their good. May they know that it will ultimately lead them to a place of blessing.

Would You guide them to seek wisdom from those who lead them? May they learn to value godly instruction and correction. May they not be led astray by the prideful hard-heartedness of others and never be guilty of rejecting correction or leading others to do the same.

May they always have tender hearts longing for holy truth.

Amen.

Generosity

A generous person will be enriched,
and the one who gives a drink of water
will receive water.

PROVERBS 11:25

Generous Giver of All Good Things,

I come today asking that You would lead my children to see the reality that they have rich lives. Regardless of their financial circumstances, my children will always be loved. May they know that You are the One who makes them very rich indeed.

May my children always be openhanded with the resources they have. May they never have clutching spirits but instead be quick to share with others in need.

May they richly experience throughout all their days the rich blessings that come from blessing others.

Amen.

Church

*Let us be concerned about one another
in order to promote love and good works,
not staying away from our worship meetings,
as some habitually do, but encouraging each other,
and all the more as you see the day drawing near.*

HEBREWS 10:24-25

Head of the Church,

I will raise my children to attend church regularly. I pray that they would find so much life, joy, hope, and meaning from attending that they will always desire that type of fellowship throughout their lives.

I realize a time will come when they will be old enough to decide for themselves whether they wish to attend church. I pray that being absent from fellowship will never become a regular pattern or habit.

In every season of their lives, may they seek out places where they can worship You corporately, be exposed to the best Bible teaching available to them, and serve You in the context of the local church.

May my children truly love Your body, Your bride.

Amen.

Rest

I think of You as I lie on my bed,
I meditate on You during the night watches.

PSALM 63:6

Our Peace and Joy,

I pray that my children will always sleep well, whether as young children, teenagers, or young adults. I pray that when they lie down, it will be with pure hearts and with minds at rest. As they reflect on each day, may they see Your intimate involvement in all their moments. As they lie awake before drifting off to sleep, may they know Your nearness.

I ask that they would never have to struggle with frequent bad dreams, night terrors, or sleeplessness. May their sleep instead be the rest of the righteous, whose hearts and minds are set on You.

Amen.

Gospel

I am not ashamed of the gospel, because it is God's
power for salvation to everyone who believes.

ROMANS 1:16

Savior,

I pray that my children's hearts would be captured at an early age by the glory of the gospel. May they first and foremost believe it and receive it for themselves. Then would You give them a passion for sharing the good news with those in their spheres of influence? May my children guide others to the salvation You offer them through faith in Your atoning sacrifice on the cross.

Would You also give them a passion for reaching all nations with Your message of hope? May they generously give of their resources to help make this happen.

May they always have a strong confidence in the power of the gospel and the grace that is offered to all who trust in You.

Amen.

Gossip

The one who reveals secrets is a constant gossip;
avoid someone with a big mouth.

PROVERBS 20:19

Lover of Truth,

Our flesh is fascinated with hearing the latest bit of gossip. Yet in our spirits, we feel the voice of Your Spirit convicting us and prompting us to walk away. I confess that often when I have heard the latest failure of someone else, it has led me in my prideful flesh to feel better about myself. This is wrong—I admit it, I repent of it, and I ask for Your forgiveness.

My children will have to deal with the same tension and struggle. May they turn to You, cry out for strength, and then resist the urge to participate in slanderous talk.

May they also choose to be wary of those they hear spreading gossip about others, knowing that such people will likely spread gossip about them as well.

May this type of sin never hold any lasting appeal for my children.

Amen.

Profession of Faith

Everyone who will acknowledge Me before men,
I will also acknowledge him before My Father in
heaven. But whoever denies Me before men, I will
also deny him before My Father in heaven.

MATTHEW 10:32-33

One I Acknowledge as My Savior and Lord,

I come today asking that my children would have a bold and shameless faith. From the moment they first recognize their need for a savior and cry out to You in repentance, may they desire for others to know they have placed their trust in You.

May they be bold in letting their family and friends, as well as their church family, know of their decision.

Throughout life, may they be willing to quickly name Your name as the hope they hold. May they be unaffected by fear, worry, or pride in proclaiming that You are their Lord.

Amen.

Parenting: Gratitude

For this boy I prayed, and the LORD has granted
me my request which I asked of Him.

1 SAMUEL 1:27, NASB

God Who Gives Good Gifts to His Children,

At times, being a parent is so much harder than I ever imagined. I love it, but it tests me in ways I have not been tested before.

In those times when I am in the deepest trenches of parenting—struggling under the weight of exhaustion, stress, frustration, and unrelenting demands—let me not forget that my children are sacred gifts from You. I asked for these gifts, and You, my blessed Father, so graciously gave them to me.

May this reminder of Your goodness to me refresh and renew my soul even today.

Amen.

Optimism

Love . . . believes all things, hopes all things.

1 CORINTHIANS 13:6-7

God Who Is Glorious and Good,

I ask that as my children love other people, they would always believe the best about them. Even though they will be disappointed at times, may my children still have hope for change and a favorable outcome.

I pray that because they are so confident in Your sovereignty and certain that You are working in all things for good, optimism would be evident in their attitudes and dispositions. May their bent be toward expecting the best of others in all situations.

Will You guide them to trust that—for themselves and others—failure is never final because You are the God who redeems and restores? May my children never be considered cynical or suspicious.

Amen.

Stillness

Be still, and know that I am God.

PSALM 46:10, NKJV

God Who Is Speaking,

This world is a loud place. Streets are filled with a steady rumble and roar. Rooms are filled with constant music, voices, and noise. Stillness is found only when we intentionally seek it.

I pray that my children would learn to treasure stillness, that they would know how to draw close and listen for Your voice in quiet moments. May they know what to do with a rainy afternoon or a lonely day that isn't crammed with activity.

In the silence, may they be at peace as You remind them of Your sovereignty and tender love.

Amen.

Health

I pray that you may prosper in every way
and be in good health physically
just as you are spiritually.

3 JOHN 1:2

Lord God, Strong and Mighty,

I pray today for the health of my children. I see clearly through Old Testament laws regarding hygiene and dietary restrictions that You care about the well-being of Your people.

I ask that Your care, blessing, and protection would be over my children on all health fronts—physical, mental, emotional, psychological, and spiritual. Would You grant them wisdom in taking care of themselves? Would You sustain them and guard them from attacks of the enemy on any of these fronts?

May nothing hinder them from serving You in the most fruitful way possible.

Amen.

Baptism

Repent . . . and be baptized, each of you,
in the name of Jesus Christ.

ACTS 2:38

One Who Has Washed My Sins Away,

When my children understand Your gospel and Your Spirit calling them to repentance, may they be quick to turn from sin to You. May they trust in You and Your finished work on Calvary.

At that time, may they also desire to be baptized—to be identified with You in Your death, burial, and resurrection. I pray that this would be a significant and meaningful experience for them and the beginning of many moments of proclaiming You publicly as their Savior and Lord.

Amen.

Marriage

[Submit] to one another in the fear of Christ.
Wives, submit to your own husbands as to the Lord. . . .
Husbands, love your wives, just as Christ loved
the church and gave Himself for her.

EPHESIANS 5:21-22, 25

Cornerstone,

As my children look around this world of adult relationships, I ask that You would bless them with the privilege of seeing holy and healthy marriages. May they see examples in their family and in the homes of friends where the husband and wife truly love and serve each other.

May the relationships they see mark them with a godly ideal of what marriage should be. Would You allow them to witness husbands and wives living out faithfulness and commitment together as they seek You, Your guidance, and Your principles for life?

I pray that even today my children's lives would be blessed by some godly examples of marriage that they can emulate should Your plan for them include a future spouse.

Amen.

Character of God:
Omniscient

*The eyes of Yahweh roam throughout the earth to show
Himself strong for those whose hearts are completely His.*

2 CHRONICLES 16:9

All-Seeing One,

Not one tiny moment of someone's life escapes Your notice. That
Your eyes see every moment of every life in every country through
all time is mind-blowing! We bow to Your omniscience.

Would You constantly find my children acting as those whose
hearts are fully Yours? May their words and deeds reflect lives that
are totally caught up and surrendered to who You are.

As a result of this, may my children experience powerful moments of Your presence and the strong hand of Your protection.
Would You grant them words of wisdom that are beyond their own?
And may they marvel at the way their lives are being led and how
perfectly You knit events together by Your wisdom and grace.

May knowing You in these powerful ways strengthen their trust.

Amen.

Wonder

The whole earth is filled with awe at your wonders;
where morning dawns, where evening fades,
you call forth songs of joy.

PSALM 65:8, NIV

One Who Will Forever Amaze Me,

Would You allow my children, throughout their days, to have hearts that can be captured by wonder? May they stand silent before a blazing sunset, fascinated by a waterfall, amazed at a star-lit midnight, in awe of how a caterpillar crawls.

All these wonders are signposts on a trail that leads seekers to You, the Creator.

May the beauty of Your handiwork always lead my children to worship You.

Amen.

Love

Love is patient, love is kind.

1 CORINTHIANS 13:4

Loving Lord,

May my children reflect You through a loving nature. I pray that their love would always demonstrate patience. May they be willing to be inconvenienced. Would You enable them to bear tiresome times without a spirit of retaliation?

May my children be kind and willing to give generously to others. I ask that You would give each of them a heart for others and a desire to actively work for the good of others.

May these qualities first and foremost show up in relationships in our home.

Amen.

Freedom from Fear

The LORD is for me; I will not be afraid.
What can man do to me?

PSALM 118:6

Our Fortress,

I ask that my children's trust in You would be a shelter against fear. Would You grow in them a faith so confident in the fact that You are almighty, all-powerful, and sovereign that many of the fears that beset other people will simply never cross my children's minds?

Even as they walk into strange, new situations, may their trust in Your nearness give them the courage and confidence that drive away fear. May a strong assurance of Your love for them give them peace each night as they sleep.

Amen.

Integrity

*Better a poor man who lives with integrity
than a rich man who distorts right and wrong.*

PROVERBS 28:6

Holy One,

You have heard me on countless occasions asking You to bless my children. I understand that blessings come in many different forms.

While I ask that You would provide for them financially to the degree that they can handle it responsibly and honor You with it, I also ask that good things would come to them as a result of leading lives of integrity.

May their reputations be sterling. May they value integrity and guard it in all times of testing.

Amen.

Prejudice

My brothers, do not show favoritism as you hold on
to the faith in our glorious Lord Jesus Christ.

JAMES 2:1

Perfect Judge,

We know You look upon the souls of all people. You are not swayed in the slightest by pigment, prestige, religious performance, or riches. One of Your attributes is Your perfect impartiality.

I pray that my children would honor You by rejecting favoritism and prejudice. May their assessment of people be based not on looks, ethnicity, wealth, or social status but on Your love for them. Would You help my children see others as lost sheep in need of You?

Amen.

Our Enemy

Be serious! Be alert! Your adversary the Devil is prowling around like a roaring lion, looking for anyone he can devour. Resist him and be firm in the faith.

1 PETER 5:8-9

Lord of Hosts,

I am so grateful for Your great power. Almighty Lord, there is no one else like You. You are able to defend us from any and all attacks.

Help me be vigilant and remember that a very real enemy is looking for opportunities to come against my children. Some of these assaults will be direct, and some will be indirect.

May the belt of truth and the shield of faith guard and protect my children. May they believe sound doctrine and be quick to call upon You. Please strengthen them to stand firm and resist the enemy always.

Amen.

Honoring Parents

*Honor your father and your mother
so that you may have a long life in the land
that the LORD your God is giving you.*

EXODUS 20:12

Our Father,

You are the God of order. You designed this world to work through authority and submission. You also designed homes to operate in the same way. In the Old Testament, the consequences for a habitually rebellious child were significant and severe.

I pray that seeds of pride and rebellion would not flourish in the hearts of my children. As they relate to their mother and me, as well as other adults, may they display humble spirits of love, trust, submission, and honor. May my children be so convinced of my love and desire for their best that a rebellious spirit would never be an issue.

For Your glory, may my children always desire to obey and honor their parents.

Amen.

Wisdom

If any of you lacks wisdom, he should ask God,
who gives to all generously and without
criticizing, and it will be given to him.

JAMES 1:5

Giver of Wisdom,

Most parents feel inadequate for the task before them. It seems You use the work of raising children as one way to keep us aware of our dependence on You.

God, I declare my need for Your wisdom as a parent.

Thank You that Your Word gives us specific principles for successfully raising children. Would You guide me to the best books and the most God-honoring teaching available that will help me apply these principles with my kids? Please keep my mind free of trendy, worldly philosophies regarding raising my children.

Help my children be patient with me. Help them forgive me when I make mistakes. May they be responsive to my guidance.

I desire to parent my children with excellence. I come asking for Your wisdom and understanding.

Amen.

Freedom from Unforgiveness

If you forgive people their wrongdoing, your heavenly
Father will forgive you as well. But if you don't forgive
people, your Father will not forgive your wrongdoing.

MATTHEW 6:14-15

Forgiving One,

Lord, I pray that once my children ask Your forgiveness for their sins, may the awe and wonder of Your grace never fade from their lives. May they demonstrate for all their days that they are overwhelmed by the mercy they have received.

In light of that wonder, may my children never consider withholding forgiveness from someone who wrongs them.

Because of Your grace, may they be quick to show grace to every offender.

Amen.

Character of God:
Holy

As the One who called you is holy,
you also are to be holy in all your conduct.

1 PETER 1:15

Holy One,

You have called us to be as You are. It is our hearts' desire to do that. Yet in this world, none of us will ever do it perfectly. We will try, and we will fail.

You want Your people to reflect Your character. This call and command rings clear in the Old Testament as well as the New Testament.

I pray that my children would strive to live holy lives by the power of Your Spirit.

May they love the things that are pure and right—in this world and in themselves.

May the world see Your reflection in my children's lives, priorities, and actions.

Amen.

Meekness

Blessed are the meek,
For they shall inherit the earth.

MATTHEW 5:5, NKJV

Suffering Servant,

Into a world of prideful people who think they are self-sufficient in their good deeds, You came in a most unexpected and unimagined way. While You could have come in blazing glory and strength, You instead came as a humble lamb that would be led to slaughter.

Your meekness was not weakness; it was great power perfectly controlled. May my children submit all their power and energy to You. Violence and vengeance have no place in the lives of Your children.

You always lead with the purest wisdom as we choose to do Your will and not our own. May my children's strength and determination be used for Your glory.

Amen.

Humor

Coarse and foolish talking or crude joking
are not suitable, but rather giving thanks.

EPHESIANS 5:4

Our Redeemer,

So much of the humor of this world is based on quickly turning an innocent phrase into one that is slightly suggestive or even out right obscene. This is a natural overflow of every heart given over to depravity and immorality.

I pray that this type of low humor would be distasteful and offensive to my children. May they laugh loud and often about things that are wholesome but not at humor that involves immorality and innuendo.

Thank You for the great joy You pour into the lives of Your people.

Amen.

Faithfulness

The fruit of the Spirit is . . . faith.

GALATIANS 5:22

Faithful One,

You have never broken a promise. You have never failed us. Your Word is secure and worthy of our trust.

We are called to be like You in this way. I pray that the hearts and lives of my children will reflect a faithfulness and loyalty to You, to family, to friends, and to those who employ them. May they always keep their promises.

May they also model a trustworthiness that is sure and dependable.

We rest in Your faithfulness, great God, and because of it, we wait with confidence for Your return.

Amen.

Forgiveness

Do not repay anyone evil for evil. Try to do
what is honorable in everyone's eyes.

ROMANS 12:17

Gracious God,

We see You on the cross, forgiving those who nailed You there. We will eternally stand in awe of this moment. Clearly only supernatural power was able to accomplish this.

I ask that Your power would flow through the lives of my children, enabling them to forgive those who hurt them instead of seeking revenge. Please help them not speak ill of those who offend them or "repay anyone evil for evil."

In their hearts, may it be enough that You see all situations and judge all events and people perfectly. Set my children's hearts at rest knowing that You will make things right in the end.

Amen.

Respect

*You are to rise in the presence of the elderly
and honor the old. Fear your God.*

LEVITICUS 19:32

Eternal God,

Pride blooms and shows itself in so many ways in our world today. One of the selfish ways it presents itself is through disrespecting the elderly.

I pray that my children would recognize that You have blessed some people with long lives. May my children's words and actions show a proper respect of the elderly.

May they always be attentive in caring for older family members, aged friends of the family, and even elderly strangers.

Amen.

Technology

"Everything is permissible," but not everything is helpful. "Everything is permissible," but not everything builds up. . . . Do everything for God's glory.

1 CORINTHIANS 10:23, 31

Giver of Wisdom,

Technology is an ever-present part of our daily lives, and each new generation is exposed to questionable and potentially harmful content at ever-younger ages. I know my children will experience the fascination of technology—we all do—but please deliver them from fixation and obsession. May they live most of their lives—and certainly the best parts of their lives—away from screens.

Would You also give them the discernment to reject the lies and illusions that social media can create? May they see the truth behind the airbrushed, filtered, and curated lives that many present in their posts. Would You deliver my children from the poison of comparison that social media fosters?

Dear God, will You protect my children from the lust of the eyes and of the flesh when they're online? Would You lead them to cry out to You for the wisdom and strength to maintain their purity? For Your glory.

Amen.

Physical Training

The training of the body has a limited benefit,
but godliness is beneficial in every way,
since it holds promise for the present life
and also for the life to come.

1 TIMOTHY 4:8

Giver of Life,

So many things in this world are good in and of themselves, and yet some people exalt their importance above what You intended. Athletics and physical training become idols for many.

If my children so desire, I want them to be involved in sports, training, and competition. Much good can be derived from these pursuits—team fellowship, the quest of striving to master a new skill, the joy of victory, and lessons in handling defeat gracefully. But Your Word says that while physical training has some limited value, spiritual training is beneficial in all areas of life.

I ask that my children would have the right perspective on the importance of athletics. May they maintain a healthy balance between things that are temporary and things that are eternal. Help me teach and model a healthy and godly balance for them. May they always give more time and attention to spiritual pursuits—cultivating strong prayer lives, understanding Your Word, and loving and serving others.

Amen.

Affection

Greet one another with a kiss of love.

1 PETER 5:14

Loving Father,

I come today asking that our home would be rich in affection. May my children see love and tenderness among family members, and may that affection give them great confidence in the security and stability of our home.

May my children be quick to express appropriate affection for their mother and me, their siblings, and their friends. In a time when so many people are starved for an arm around their shoulder or a reassuring hug, may my children know the power they have to express care for others.

May it always be sincere, appropriate, and pure.

Amen.

Discernment

Grow in the grace and knowledge
of our Lord and Savior Jesus Christ.

2 PETER 3:18

God Who Is the Truth,

This world overwhelms us with a steady barrage of messages—some subtle, some overt.

I pray my children will grow in their knowledge of You, that they might be able to clearly discern which messages are in harmony with Your Word and which messages are antagonistic toward Your nature.

May they develop great skill in rightly discerning Your truth so they will easily recognize half-truths and lies.

Amen.

Growing Socially

Jesus increased . . . in favor with . . . people.

LUKE 2:52

Triune God,

You are perfect in all the ways You relate to people. Yet for us, who are born into this broken world, learning grace and social skills is a process.

I pray that my children would mature well socially. May they learn how to relate to people of all age groups in ways that are respectful, caring, and appropriate. May they earn respect and admiration from everyone they interact with.

Would You guide them to always maintain a beautiful, simple childlikeness and never behave in childish ways?

Amen.

God's Word

*I have treasured the words of [God's] mouth
more than my daily food.*

JOB 23:12

God Who Is Not Silent,

I ask today that my children would always treasure Your Word. May they value the perfect and pure riches of Your self-revelation to us.

Would You give them a passion for Your Word? May they long to read it, hear it, learn from it, memorize it, live it, and even teach it.

I pray that my life will convey to them my belief that it is a holy treasure of unfathomable wealth.

Thank You for Your Word.

Amen.

Death

Even though I walk through the valley
of the shadow of death,
I fear no evil, for You are with me.

PSALM 23:4, NASB

Lord of Life,

At some point, my children will encounter death for the first time. It might be the death of a favorite animal, a friend of the family, or perhaps a family member. Whenever it happens—as toddlers, teenagers, or even young adults—it will be an unsettling event in their lives.

They will have questions. They will see sadness. They may even feel fear. I pray that the peace and hope we have in our relationship with You will be an extraordinary comfort to them in that time.

Would You even now prepare my children for that encounter by grounding them in Your truth about what happens at death? Would You guard their hearts and minds from abnormal fears anytime they think of it? Would You use any experience of grief to cultivate empathy in their lives? May they bring You glory by showing compassion toward others who grieve.

Amen.

Joy

I greatly rejoice in the LORD,
I exult in my God.

ISAIAH 61:10

Giver of Joy,

I pray that Your joy would overflow in my children's lives in spite of difficult circumstances they experience along the way.

I ask that they would not develop a pattern of becoming sullen, moody, withdrawn, angry, distressed, or sad whenever life is hard. Would You use these dark periods to draw them even closer to You? Please teach them that they can find joy in You, even when skies are gray.

May my children not base their outlook on their current circumstances. At best, this would ensure only brief periods of happiness. May they instead know the richer, deeper, and enduring joy that comes from fixing their gaze on You no matter what life brings their way.

Amen.

Courage

Be alert, stand firm in the faith,
act like a man, be strong.
1 CORINTHIANS 16:13

Almighty and Everlasting God,

Throughout Scripture, Your call and command went out, particularly to great leaders, to be strong and courageous. My children will surely face situations that will require great courage.

Would You prepare them now for that time? Would You guide them to learn the importance of keeping their eyes fixed on You instead of on the difficulties they are facing?

As they recall that You are almighty, all-knowing, all-powerful, all-wise, faithful, holy, good, and sovereign, may it fan the flame of confidence within them to step into the places You are leading them.

Amen.

Future

Seek first the kingdom of God and His righteousness,
and all [you need] will be provided for you.
Therefore don't worry about tomorrow,
because tomorrow will worry about itself.

MATTHEW 6:33-34

Our Omnipotent God,

Some people just seem prone to worry, especially as they consider what could possibly go wrong tomorrow.

I pray that this would not be true of my children. Though the future is filled with many uncertainties, may they face it trusting that You are leading them into educational pursuits, relationships, and places of employment and service You have prepared for them.

May they be confident that Your mercies will be new each morning. May they trust that You will show them grace for each and every day of their lives. May they find great peace and confidence in trusting that all their tomorrows are already in Your hand.

Amen.

Creativity

Our Lord and God,
You are worthy to receive
glory and honor and power,
because You have created all things,
and because of Your will
they exist and were created.

REVELATION 4:11

Great Creator,

The first thing we know about You in Scripture is that You are a creator. Our world overflows with colors, sights, sounds, and scents—countless things that show us how original and inspired You are.

I know my children, created in Your image, have a creative side. It may show itself in different forms throughout different seasons of their lives, but I pray that You would protect it. Guard my children from voices and influences that might seek to discourage them and cause them to lose heart in their artistic endeavors.

I pray that their artistic expressions will glorify You and reflect to the world all that is good, pure, right, and true. For Your glory.

Amen.

Lord's Supper

This is My body. . . . This is My blood. . . .
I assure you: I will no longer drink of the fruit
of the vine until that day when I drink it
in a new way in the kingdom of God.

MARK 14:22, 24-25

Lamb of God and Coming King,

I pray that every opportunity my children have to partake in the Lord's Supper would be approached with great anticipation, reverence, and respect. May they always examine themselves before taking part, as You instruct us in Your Word. May Your table be a special and intimate moment of worship for them.

I pray that time at Your table will always move my children to deep gratitude for Your great sacrifice on their behalf.

I also ask that it would leave them with tremendous hope and anticipation for those moments when, as You promised, we will share the cup with You in Your Kingdom. What joy!

Amen.

Love

The one who has My commands and keeps
them is the one who loves Me.

JOHN 14:21

Worthy One,

I pray that love might richly and lavishly flow from my children's lives. May their love for others be expressed through caring, sharing, listening, giving affection, sacrificing, and speaking words of truth and life.

When it comes to You, may their love be shown through rich and deep worship and adoration. Most of all, may they consistently express their love for You through obedience. May their trust in You, their love for Your Word, and their desire to please You be reflected in how quickly they do whatever You call them to do.

Would You lead them to make this their daily offering of love to You?

Amen.

Freedom

*Now the Lord is the Spirit, and where the Spirit
of the Lord is, there is freedom.*

2 CORINTHIANS 3:17

Giver of True Freedom,

I pray that my children would have the hearts of patriots. May they passionately love this land, defend it, want the best for it, and pray for its leaders. May they truly appreciate the high cost that has been paid by so many for the liberties we enjoy. May they always honor those who have sacrificed to secure and maintain our freedom. May they never take that freedom for granted.

Would You grow in my children a deeper appreciation of the greater liberty You secured for Your people at the Cross?

May their love and devotion for this nation be eclipsed only by their worship and adoration of You.

Amen.

Faith

Without faith it is impossible to please God,
for the one who draws near to Him must believe that
He exists and rewards those who seek Him.

HEBREWS 11:6

The God We Will One Day See,

I pray that my children would truly trust and believe that though there are things we can't see, they are real nonetheless. May they have faith in the reality of Your Kingdom, where You reign even now over all things.

May they not simply believe in the existence of a divine being but have a deep and abiding faith that You, the God of all creation, the God of Holy Scripture, the One who revealed Yourself to us in Jesus, the God who reigns now in heaven and on earth, are indeed the one true God.

May they believe that Your Son is the Way, the Truth, and the Life; that Scripture is perfect and sufficient for all things; that their lives have meaning and purpose; and that they will one day stand before You.

May my children experience the reward of those who seek passionately after You: forgiveness, righteousness, and heavenly blessings.

Amen.

Stewardship of Treasure

On the first day of the week,
each of you is to set something aside
and save in keeping with how he prospers.

1 CORINTHIANS 16:2

Our Generous God,

I pray that my children would always believe that every penny they earn is actually a gift from You. May they also realize that even though they hold the money in their hands, it in fact still belongs to You.

From that right perspective, would You guide my children to always be regular, willing, grateful, and joyful givers? May they see all giving as a meaningful act of worship to You.

Lord, would You lead my children, even from a young age, to be faithful in stewarding the little they have so that You may one day entrust them with more?

Amen.

Reconciliation

If you are offering your gift on the altar,
and there you remember that your brother
has something against you, leave your gift there
in front of the altar. First go and be reconciled with
your brother, and then come and offer your gift.

MATTHEW 5:23-24

Our Reconciler,

I pray that my children would have a special sensitivity regarding the condition of their relationships. May they be aware when something is not quite right or is unresolved with a friend. May they never pretend that everything is okay or deny it when things aren't quite right. May they find it impossible to joyfully serve You while failing to attend to the problem.

Whether the wrong is real or imagined, may my children be strong enough and humble enough to take the initiative with the other person. I pray that through Your grace, they would be able to express what they feel and find mercy, understanding, and restoration. When this occurs, would You bless the relationship going forward and encourage both parties to not let offenses go unaddressed?

Amen.

Reputation

A good name is to be chosen over great wealth;
favor is better than silver and gold.

PROVERBS 22:1

Name above All Names,

I pray that my children would care about having a good reputation. I ask this not that it may feed any fleshly pride within them but rather so that they will reflect You with their lives.

I pray that my children would pursue excellence all their days. May this show itself in their work ethic, their speech, their scholastic achievements, their relationships, and their self-discipline. May it cause people to take a closer look at my children's lives and the motivation behind all they do.

May this always lead to opportunities to make You known.

Amen.

Gentleness

The fruit of the Spirit is . . . gentleness.

GALATIANS 5:22-23

Gentle Shepherd,

Everyone knows the tension and turmoil created from being around a child who is out of control. The defiance and lack of submission can cause great uneasiness for those nearby.

I pray that my children would display meek and gentle spirits. Though they are strong within, may that strength show itself in winsome and controlled ways.

Would You let their gentle dispositions create great ease and enjoyment for those around them?

Amen.

Youth

Remember your Creator in the days of your youth:
Before the days of adversity come.

ECCLESIASTES 12:1

The One Who Gives Life Meaning,

Youth can be a barrier that hinders some from finding faith in You. In youth, so many temporal joys and distractions can keep people from asking the deeper questions of life.

I pray that my children would come to You at a young age. I ask that Your truth would arrest their hearts and gain their whole attention, focus, and devotion. Then, with the most active and productive years ahead, may they have abundant opportunities to do work that gives You glory.

In old age, many who don't trust You are surrounded by loneliness and bitterness, trapped in the pain and regret of unfulfilled lives. I pray that as they grow older, my children will enjoy the peace, joy, and blessings of fruitful lives because they trusted in You when they were young.

Amen.

Siblings

Show family affection to one another with brotherly
love. Outdo one another in showing honor.

ROMANS 12:10

Heavenly Father,

The greatest outward evidence of being Yours is the way we love others. I want our home to overflow with love. Today I come before You praying that my children would truly love one another.

May they be caring, giving, and compassionate toward each other. May affection be real and frequently expressed among them. May they cherish the bonds they share. Would You help them see themselves not just as siblings but as the dearest, closest friends? May their relationships reflect peace, kindness, and enjoyment of one another.

Would You help my children's lives and relationships with one another give evidence that they share not just earthly parents but also a heavenly Father?

Amen.

Wisdom

Wisdom is supreme—so get wisdom.
And whatever else you get, get understanding.

PROVERBS 4:7

All-Wise One,

No one accidentally becomes wise. For all who acquire wisdom, it is the ongoing, passionate pursuit of their lives.

I pray that my children, from an early age, would realize that some people live life in a way that seems smarter and better than the way others live. May they see that this blessing comes from following Your instructions.

I pray that my children's hearts would be set to seek wisdom. May it be a daily determination to chase after Your higher ways. May this passion for wisdom not only lead them deeper into Your Word, but may it drive them toward excellent authors and teachers and keep them away from much of the secular folly and drivel that passes for wisdom today.

Amen.

Conduct

Conduct yourselves honorably among the Gentiles,
so that in a case where they speak against you
as those who do what is evil, they will, by
observing your good works, glorify God.

1 PETER 2:12

Holy and Perfect One,

I pray that my children would mirror You in their behavior. I ask that their examples would draw the attention of unbelievers. I pray that You would cause people to notice that they are somehow different. May the difference be the authentic love and care my children display for all people.

May my children also project a radiant joy and hope that are appealing to others. I pray that their lives are so rich with deeds of love and humble service that nonbelievers will notice how different they are in this self-centered world.

May they live for Your glory, and may their lives and examples compel others to do the same.

Amen.

Future Vocation

Do you see a man skilled in his work?
He will stand in the presence of kings.
He will not stand in the presence of unknown men.

PROVERBS 22:29

God Who Leads Us,

I believe You have great dreams and plans for my children. I believe You have meaningful, purposeful work for them that will glorify Your name. I trust that You have uniquely designed each of them for this place of service and will call them to it.

May they seek after You diligently, listening for Your leading so they will find work that is fulfilling and joyful. Please guide me now as I do what I can to equip them with character, skills, and values that will help them excel in the career paths they choose.

I pray that their future work would provide well for them, but more than that, I desire that their work would open doors for them to join You in Your mission of redemption in this world.

Amen.

Character of God: Good

The LORD is good.

NAHUM 1:7

Good and Gracious One,

You are good. In all You say, in all You do, You are good and perfect. In Your nature, in Your essence, You are good. All Your decrees, all Your creation—all of it is good!

May my children believe that they are indeed among the good works You created for Your pleasure. May they also be aware of Your goodness to them in countless ways in this physical world—in beauty, scents, colors, tastes, music. May my children live with deep and enduring gratitude to You for the wonderful gift of salvation that You offer them.

Would You guide my children to respond to Your goodness with worship, faith, and adoration?

Amen.

Love

Love your neighbor as yourself.

MARK 12:31

Lover of the Unworthy,

To truly love You, we cannot have hearts for You alone. To love You means letting Your love and care overflow to all those around us.

I ask today that my children would deeply, intentionally, and purposefully love the people they encounter. May their love not simply be emotional or sentimental, but may it be active in meeting the needs of others. May they show evidence of loving You by loving others with helpful, caring, and compassionate spirits. I pray that this would be a top priority.

I ask that they would not be selective or prejudiced in the way they love. May they love everyone, not just those they like and enjoy hanging out with. Would You teach them to love even their enemies—just as You did with us?

Amen.

Parenting: Guidance

Don't stir up anger in your children, but bring
them up in the training and instruction of the Lord.

EPHESIANS 6:4

Heavenly Father,

I ask for Your help that I may lead, train, and teach my children well without exasperating them. Please restrain me from punishing them out of anger, but rather help me see moments of rebelliousness as opportunities to instruct and train my children in wisdom.

May I never express anything that resembles favoritism among my children. The biblical account of Esau and Jacob shows the devastating consequences of this.

Please curb any tendency to set unrealistic expectations for my children or to push them to achieve beyond reasonable limits. Keep me from crippling my children by making them bear the intense pressure of trying to please an overbearing parent.

Would You give my children responsive and teachable spirits that are eager to learn? Perfect Father, protect their hearts from any harmful effects of my imperfect instruction. I pray that when I correct them, they would receive my discipline and learn the lessons You want them to learn. May this grow good fruit in their lives.

I need Your Word, Your Spirit, and Your wisdom to do the job You have called me to do. Please lead me, fill me, and use me.

Amen.

Remembering

At night I remember my music;
I meditate in my heart, and my spirit ponders.

PSALM 77:6

Faithful in All Seasons,

Though I would not wish it for my children, I accept that in days ahead, they will face times of trial, valleys of loneliness, and dark nights when You seem to be distant. I pray that in those times, my children will remember well Your faithfulness!

May they remember how faithful You have been throughout their lives. May they remember how Your promises have always proved to be true. May they remember that You have never left them alone but have always provided good things for them.

Would You guide their thoughts so that those memories will give them comfort and strength to endure the hard times?

Amen.

Zeal

Never be lacking in zeal, but keep your
spiritual fervor, serving the Lord.

ROMANS 12:11, NIV

Our Intentional God,

Your Word instructs us to do everything with all our might. I pray that my children would believe passionately in whatever they take on, especially spiritual pursuits.

May they wholeheartedly tackle the projects before them and work with enthusiasm and excellence. May they trust that You know and see all things and that You care about details.

May my children's fervent spirits be a joy to their instructors, and may their diligence inspire those around them to pursue excellence. I pray that they would never be lazy or indifferent but zealous about whatever they do. And may they do it all for Your glory.

Amen.

Confession

When I kept silent, my bones became brittle
from my groaning all day long. . . .
Then I acknowledged my sin to You
and did not conceal my iniquity.
I said,
"I will confess my transgressions to the LORD,"
and You took away the guilt of my sin.

PSALM 32:3, 5

Faithful Forgiver,

When my children sin, I want them to quickly feel the weight of Your hand upon their hearts. May their spirits stay tender toward You so that conviction will lead to confession right away.

Thank You for the assurance of grace and forgiveness whenever we confess our faithlessness to You. The certainty of Your love for us is such a kindness, and it is Your kindness that leads us to repentance.

May my children richly bless You for the mercy and cleansing they find when they confess their sin to You. May they never live an extended period of time with guilt pressing down on them.

Amen.

Friends

Iron sharpens iron,
and one man sharpens another.

PROVERBS 27:17

Our Refiner,

While I pray that throughout their lives my children will always have good and godly companions, today I am petitioning for them to have *faithful* friends, particularly during the difficult years of middle school and high school.

I pray that You would bring good friends their way—specifically *best friends* who would be a blessing and a constant presence in my children's lives. I pray that these friendships would be mutually beneficial. May they encourage each other to be better people and more faithful to You.

May their conversations on intellectual or spiritual matters help them develop sharper minds and a more certain faith. May the faithfulness of these relationships be a source of great comfort and joy.

Amen.

Testimony

You are a chosen race, a royal priesthood,
a holy nation, a people for His possession,
so that you may proclaim the praises
of the One who called you out of darkness
into His marvelous light.

1 PETER 2:9

God Who Defines Me,

I come asking today, in light of this passage, that my children would not see their identities in light of their accomplishments. Instead, may they always know that they are part of a chosen, holy people belonging to You. May this define who they are and how they see themselves.

May they live with an overwhelming awareness of the life You've called them to. But would You also help them remember the lives You've called them *from*? I pray that this awareness would keep a steady flame of joy and gratitude burning within their souls.

I want my children to be faithful in declaring Your praise. May they also declare Your praises and Your truth to those who don't know You yet.

Amen.

Authority

Bondservants, be obedient to those who are your
masters according to the flesh, with fear and
trembling, in sincerity of heart, as to Christ.

EPHESIANS 6:5, NKJV

God Who Is Present at All Times,

At some point, my children will start their first jobs. They will answer to adults other than their parents. I pray my children would be mindful that when they serve an employer, they are also serving You. May they do it well.

I ask that my children would demonstrate respect and obedience to those in charge. May their diligence and manners win them favor with their supervisors. May they be faithful to pursue excellence in all aspects of their work.

Would You bless them, protect them, and guard them as they encounter new people and influences in their places of employment?

Amen.

Lying

Truthful lips endure forever,
but a lying tongue, only a moment.

PROVERBS 12:19

One Who Is Truth,

All children are tempted to stretch the truth from time to time. Just like the first lie Adam told in the Garden of Eden, it's usually to avoid consequences.

I pray today that the first few times my children tell a lie, the consequences would convince them that they don't want to lie anymore. I'm praying not simply for outward compliance, Lord, but for You to change their hearts. Would You help them see and believe that truth is the foundation for all good relationships?

As my children grow, Father, may they see how friendships based on truth telling are ones that endure.

Amen.

Stealing

Ill-gotten gains do not profit anyone,
but righteousness rescues from death.

PROVERBS 10:2

Giver of Good Things,

I know that at some point, my children will be tempted to take shortcuts by cheating in some way, or even stealing. I pray that they would not give in to temptation, but if they do steal, may it be on a small scale and happen while they are young. I also ask that their wrongdoing would be revealed quickly and lead to a teachable moment they will never forget.

Lord, would You use that experience to impress upon my children the regret that comes when we take what isn't ours? Let them come away from it with a strong desire not to ever cheat or steal again. May they acknowledge that Your ways are better, higher, and wiser, and always lead to life.

Amen.

Conduct

Let no one despise your youth; instead, you should
be an example to the believers in . . . conduct.

1 TIMOTHY 4:12

Giver of Life,

You not only gave us life, but You also showed us through Your
Son how to live it to the fullest. I pray that my children would value
being good examples of those who are led by Your Word and Your
Spirit. May the choices they make reflect that You are their Lord.

I pray that they would desire to emulate the qualities they see
in Your life and Your earthly ministry. Please protect them and
prevent them from living hypocritical lifestyles of saying one thing
with their lips and another with their choices.

May their lives strongly reflect Your example.

Amen.

Golden Rule

Just as you want others to do for you,
do the same for them.

LUKE 6:31

The One Who Is Love,

I ask that today's verse would be a guiding passage for my children's lives. May their general attitude toward everyone they encounter be characterized by love. I pray that in every interaction, they would ask themselves, *How can I show love to this person?*

May my children be known for being generous and always finding ways to express care for the people around them. I pray that they would be quick to show sincere love in their words and acts of service. Would You teach them to be selfless and always focus on the well-being of others instead of the way others treat them?

May my children be committed to expressing love even if others do not love them in return.

Amen.

Kindness

Therefore, God's chosen ones,
holy and loved, put on . . . kindness.

COLOSSIANS 3:12

King of Compassion,

I want the evidence of Your character to shine in the lives of my children. A major way others will see Your image will be in the general kindness my children display.

May they truly be as concerned for the welfare of others as they are for themselves. May their kindness show itself in words and deeds of compassion.

It is Your kindness, Lord, that leads us to repentance. I pray that the kindness of my children will draw out the best from others. May they be especially kind not only to their family and friends but also to strangers they meet.

Amen.

Missions

Go, therefore, and make disciples of all nations,
baptizing them in the name of the Father and of the Son
and of the Holy Spirit, teaching them to observe
everything I have commanded you. And remember,
I am with you always, to the end of the age.

MATTHEW 28:19-20

Immanuel,

I pray that my children would be disciple-makers. May their great passion be to see people come to faith in You and grow into mature, fruitful, serving ministers. May my children have a deep love for Your Word and for sharing its riches with others.

At an appropriate time, I pray that You would place a burden on my children's hearts to see an unbeliever they know come to faith. May our entire family be diligent to pray toward this end and to speak truth as we have the opportunity. Would You allow us the privilege and joy of seeing this person come to saving faith? And may the joy and the holy blessing of it all make a deep impression on my children and be a significant part of their stories.

Thank You that as my children serve You, they can have the confidence and certainty of Your presence with them always. My children are Yours to use for Your glory.

Amen.

Persecution

If you are ridiculed for the name of Christ,
you are blessed, because the Spirit
of glory and of God rests on you.

1 PETER 4:14

Worthy One,

I have prayed often for my children to have a strong and certain faith that would be clearly out of step with the prevailing culture. I understand that this means some people will dislike and seek to persecute my children.

I pray in those times, Lord, that my children will find the strength and grace to handle any insult or mistreatment. May they faithfully endure and be protected and guarded by Your hand. May Your Spirit fill them with power and wisdom in those moments. May they boldly hold to and proclaim their faith.

May they know the special blessing of Your approval and satisfaction with them whenever they experience persecution.

Amen.

Gratitude

Give thanks in everything,
for this is God's will for you.

1 THESSALONIANS 5:18

Sovereign One,

You command us to give thanks in all things. This is possible only if we trust that You are at work in every situation—through even the most difficult, trying, and disappointing circumstances.

I pray that my children would develop hearts of gratitude. I pray that You would bring them to maturity so that they will be able to thank You for the lessons You teach them during difficult times.

May they experience the many ways You bring blessing out of hardship. I ask that this would increase their ability to trust You the next time difficulties come their way. Would You help my children express their thanks to You even in the lonely, sad, and uncertain seasons of life?

Amen.

Church

LORD, I love the house where You dwell,
the place where Your glory resides.

PSALM 26:8

Head of the Church,

There is so much to love about Your church. It is the place Your Word is clearly and regularly proclaimed. It is where Your people gather together to worship and adore You. It is the primary means by which believers meet to encourage one another.

I pray that my children would love everything about Your church, as I do. May they have great anticipation for gathering with Your people. I ask that they would look forward to the chance to worship You. Would You bless them with sincere and godly teachers and leaders along the way?

Would You give my children hearts of love for Your body, Lord?

Amen.

School

Instruct a wise man,
and he will be wiser still.

PROVERBS 9:9

Lord of Every Season,

I know that You can powerfully use a new school year to write another chapter in my children's stories. The beginning of each year is like a gift to be unwrapped—full of new teachers, new friendships and relationships, new subjects and topics to be explored, new learning opportunities, and new challenges.

As this new year approaches, my first concern is for the safety of my children. Whatever classrooms they are in, please keep them physically safe. And please protect them spiritually from any godless and false ideas they might encounter. Don't allow any lies to take root within them.

May all my children's teachers have hearts that genuinely care for the welfare of their students. I pray that every teacher would demonstrate patience with each child and encourage students to excel.

Amen.

Temptation

*Each person is tempted when he is drawn away
and enticed by his own evil desires. Then after
desire has conceived, it gives birth to sin, and when
sin is fully grown, it gives birth to death.*

JAMES 1:14-15

Tester of Our Faith,

I know You test our faith to see just how much we depend on You. You never tempt us, but You do allow the enemy to present us with temptations that we can only overcome by trusting and obeying You.

My children have unique weaknesses that the enemy will try to exploit. Whether these weaknesses are due to environment, upbringing, sinful tendencies, or personal choices, they are doorways through which temptation enters their lives. Temptation always promises something enjoyable when in fact, it causes harm.

I pray that You would strengthen my children for the battles they face. Please give them hearts that are passionate about holiness and purity. May my children be committed to standing strong against temptation. When opportunities for evil present themselves, may my kids take immediate action to overcome them. Please help them, Father.

Amen.

Forgiveness

*Therefore, God's chosen ones, . . . put on
heartfelt compassion, . . . accepting one another
and forgiving one another if anyone has a complaint
against another. Just as the Lord has forgiven
you, so you must also forgive.*

COLOSSIANS 3:12-13

Giver of Grace,

At some point, friends will say things that hurt my children's feelings. Others will do things to cause them embarrassment or even harm. I pray that my children would be so confident in the grace they have been shown that they would feel no need to reciprocate. May they faithfully endure the wrongs that come their way.

May the seeds of resentment never find a home within their hearts. May my children instead be quick to forgive those who offend them.

Amen.

Parenting: Guidance

Unless the LORD builds a house,
its builders labor over it in vain.

PSALM 127:1

Perfect Father,

I desire for You to be intimately involved with our family. I seek Your wisdom and leading in each area and detail of our homelife and relationships. I declare my need for You and Your wisdom.

Jesus, would You be the foundation of our home? I pray that my children would see You as the Builder of our lives, individually and as a family. Enable them to see Your hand at work in our family and seek Your wisdom and leading in their lives as well.

Father, we want our family to endure—not just to survive, but to thrive and flourish more and more as years go by. This is possible only if we follow Your plans for how to "do" life and family well.

Amen.

Music

Speaking to one another
in psalms, hymns, and spiritual songs,
singing and making music
from your heart to the Lord.

EPHESIANS 5:19

Giver of All Good Things,

I pray that music would have a special place in my children's lives. Because of the joy and hope they have in You, I pray that their hearts would often overflow with song. May it be evidence of lives filled with Your Spirit.

I pray that my children would be drawn to music that is excellent and honoring to You. May they not only enjoy new music that reflects truth and beauty, but may they also appreciate quality music that has endured through the centuries.

May they sing to You in public as well as in private. Would You even give them an interest in playing an instrument?

May music be a rich and rewarding experience throughout their lives. May the music they make be a blessing to them and especially to You.

Amen.

Self-Control

A fool gives full vent to his anger,
but a wise man holds it in check.

PROVERBS 29:11

Strength for the Weak,

It is a comfort to see in Your Word that even You get angry. We get angry often. But the difference is that You are perfect and we are not. We need Your strength and wisdom in those times when anger rises in our hearts.

I pray that my children would exercise great self-control over how they express their anger. Please guard them from explosive outbursts that give full vent to their anger. Protect them from saying or doing things they might regret later.

I ask that instead they would consider how to respond in a godly way. May they take responsibility for their feelings and also express grace toward those they are angry with.

Amen.

God's Word

Your word is a lamp for my feet
and a light on my path.

PSALM 119:105

Light of the World,

You are the Great Shepherd who guides us through our days. You give us warnings to protect us from dangers, and You lead us into good places of blessing. Your Word shines truth on the road before us.

May my children love Your Word and in wisdom heed the warnings You give them. May this lead them to walk in ways that keep them far from sin. May they trust Your Word and the path it reveals before them. Would You guide them to follow that light into ways of righteousness?

Instill within my children a great passion for Your truth so that they may walk without stumbling.

Amen.

Reverence

Since we are receiving a kingdom
that cannot be shaken, let us hold on to grace.
By it, we may serve God acceptably, with reverence
and awe, for our God is a consuming fire.

HEBREWS 12:28-29

God on High,

I pray that through conversations at home, Bible study, and all the instruction my children will absorb during their formative years, they would develop a high view of who You are. May they have a deep respect and reverence for You. May a healthy, holy fear for You color their days.

Please lead them to esteem You as the one true God who reigns from heaven with power and authority and will one day perfectly judge all people. As they consider who You are, may it lead to a deep awe that You would pursue a relationship with them.

May this wonder and worship, along with the desire for intimacy with You, keep them growing in a rich relationship with You throughout their lives.

Amen.

Love

*God loved the world in this way: He gave His One
and Only Son, so that everyone who believes in
Him will not perish but have eternal life.*

JOHN 3:16

Lord of Love,

People, events, and circumstances in my children's lives will
convey different ideas of what love is. Many books, movies, and
songs will give them a skewed or false understanding of love.

But Your sacrifice on the cross is the only true definition of *love*.
I pray that my children would embrace that picture of love. May
they clearly see that You initiated a relationship with us. May they
be in wonder at the lengths to which You went in redeeming us—
even laying down Your own life!

May this vision of self-sacrifice for the good of others be the ideal
of love they strive to emulate through the power of Your Spirit.

Amen.

Resisting Sin

If you do not do what is right, sin is crouching at the door. Its desire is for you, but you must rule over it.

GENESIS 4:7

Strong Tower,

I pray that as my children grow in their faith, they would not be naive regarding the spiritual battles they will face in life. May they come to understand that they have a real enemy who will try to thwart Your plans by bringing dishonor and even harm to them. May this reality not frighten my children but instead motivate them to prayerfulness and sober, holy living.

Would You convince my children that even a small degree of evil or compromise is a serious matter? May the biblical metaphor of a roaring lion in search of prey to devour impress on them the reality and danger of their adversary.

I pray that my children would depend on You in this battle, crying out to You for strength to overcome the temptations before them. May they experience countless moments of victory that will bring You great glory.

Amen.

Justice

[The Lord] has told you . . .
what it is [He] requires of you:
to act justly,
to love faithfulness,
and to walk humbly with your God.

MICAH 6:8

God of Justice,

Everything You do is perfect and right. We cry out for Your Kingdom to come, because we long for a time when there will be no injustice and everything will be as it should be.

I pray that my children would have hearts of mercy for the downtrodden of this world. May they care deeply about the poor and afflicted, as well as for orphans and widows. Would You move them to give freely of their time in bringing comfort and relief to those in need?

As my children walk through this world, may they live out their days with humble hearts expressed in a right relationship with You and others.

Amen.

Anxiety

Don't worry about anything, but in everything,
through prayer and petition with thanksgiving,
let your requests be made known to God.

PHILIPPIANS 4:6

God Who Is Near,

There will be times when a wave of worry will wash over my children—an upcoming test, a big sports competition, an uncomfortable situation they find themselves in. I pray that You and I will have adequately prepared them to handle such moments.

May they trust that You have led them *to* these moments and will lead them *through* each one. As they focus their attention on Your sovereignty and power, would Your peace that is beyond all human understanding reign in their hearts and minds?

In moments of anxiety, may they be quick to run to You and pour out their concerns.

Amen.

Sickness

I will bring you health
and will heal you of your wounds—
this is the LORD's declaration.

JEREMIAH 30:17

Our Healer,

Times of sickness or disease will impact nearly every child. While I might wish this were not true, I pray that when my children experience illnesses or injuries, You will bring healing. Ultimately, I entrust my children into Your loving hands and know that whatever You allow in their lives, You are able to work it for good. In asking for Your healing, I also pray that You would use times of illness to deepen their faith and develop godly character in their lives.

When my children need medical care, Father, lead us to excellent and compassionate health care professionals. May my children be patient and diligent in taking their medicine and wise in getting the rest they need. I pray that they would have positive experiences with doctors, nurses, and dentists and not fear them.

We acknowledge that You alone can bring true healing, and we thank You for Your healing touch.

Amen.

Character of God: Faithful

Know that Yahweh your God is God,
the faithful God who keeps His gracious covenant
loyalty for a thousand generations with those
who love Him and keep His commands.

DEUTERONOMY 7:9

Faithful One,

You are gloriously perfect in faithfulness. In a world where promises are broken and people's words are no longer their bond, You are always completely true to Your word and Your promises. Your Holy Book is filled with stories of Your faithfulness to Your people.

I pray that Your example would stir up great confidence in the hearts of my children. May it lead them to ever-increasing faith in the trustworthiness of Your Word. May they cling tightly to the certainty that You will fulfill all Your promises.

Amen.

Physical Growth

Jesus increased in . . . stature.

LUKE 2:52

The One Who Knit Us Together,

It is amazing that Your Holy Word talks about the physical growth of Your Son as a child here on earth. With that in mind, I pray now for healthy growth for my own children.

May all their senses, systems, and faculties develop well and appropriately. May their minds be sharp and clear. Would You give them a love for physical activity and recreation and help them make healthy nutritional choices?

Would You protect them from the enemy's attempts to sabotage their physical health and growth? May their bodies serve them well as they serve You.

Amen.

Purity

Run from sexual immorality!

1 CORINTHIANS 6:18

Wise and Holy One,

I ask that even from a young age, my children would make wise decisions about guarding their sexual purity. May they be committed to Your ideal—that the incredible gift of sex belongs only within the context of marriage.

May they set firm boundaries to protect not only their bodies but their minds and spirits as well. In moments of temptation, would You sustain and empower them to resist and run from immorality?

May they be strong and secure enough in themselves, and in Your love and my love, that no opportunity to give themselves away before marriage will seem worth it.

Please keep them safe from perversion or any predator that might be part of the enemy's plan to destroy them. May any attack be completely crushed before it even presents itself!

May my children experience in marriage the rich blessings of sexual intimacy.

Amen.

Peacemaking

The fruit of righteousness is sown in peace
by those who cultivate peace.

JAMES 3:18

Our True Peace,

I pray that my children would be sensitive to tension in their relationships and that they would act as peacemakers. May they be well respected and trusted so that others feel safe telling them what's wrong.

Would You guide my children with great wisdom in these times? May they faithfully seek Your counsel, and may they be able to help others find a grace-filled solution to the problem.

I ask that even from a young age, my children would be peacemakers in their relationships with siblings and friends.

Amen.

Perseverance

Since we also have such a large cloud of witnesses
surrounding us, let us . . . run with endurance
the race that lies before us.

HEBREWS 12:1

Author and Perfecter of Our Faith,

I pray that my children would have strong, determined spirits. May they even be stubborn and unmovable when they know a cause is right.

I pray that their faith would always be in forward motion, persevering through every obstacle. Even though at times they will stumble and make mistakes, may they gain great wisdom from their failures and learn strategies to avoid making the same mistakes next time. Even when they fall, may they fall forward, growing stronger through the experience.

May they be determined to press on, forgetting what lies behind and reaching for what is ahead, never slowing down and never giving up.

Amen.

Reading

*[The righteous man delights] in the LORD's instruction,
and he meditates on it day and night.*

PSALM 1:2

Living Word,

I know the priority You place on Your people spending time in
Your Word. I agree that it's important. I want my children to delight
in reading Your Word. I come before You asking that You would
help them become good readers.

May they always love reading books and learning. If at some
point they find reading difficult, would You show me the best way
to help them? I ask that they would be diligent in overcoming these
difficulties and even exceed the skill levels for their age groups.

The brain—and how we learn—is a wondrous, miraculous part
of Your design. Would You enable my children to excel in reading
so they might fully enjoy time in Your Word?

Amen.

Worship

*Therefore, brothers, by the mercies of God,
I urge you to present your bodies as a living sacrifice,
holy and pleasing to God; this is your spiritual worship.*

ROMANS 12:1

Worthy One,

In times of worshiping You, my children may offer up a prayer. Or they may offer a song, a word of praise, or even their tithes and offerings. Yet of all the things they offer, I pray that first and foremost they would offer themselves to You—body, mind, emotions, and will.

In light of who You are and the countless, indescribable mercies You have shown them, this will be a reasonable and right response on their part. May they daily offer all they are to You and actively seek to be used in any way You desire.

May they see incredible things happen in their lives as they offer themselves to You, and may this be evidence that You are indeed Lord over all. For Your glory always.

Amen.

Evangelism

The fruit of the righteous is a tree of life,
And he who wins souls is wise.

PROVERBS 11:30, NKJV

God Who Seeks and Saves,

I pray that my children would live with an awareness that people around them every day are looking for meaning in their lives and for answers to the difficulties they face. May my children take advantage of the opportunities they have to speak of the hope they have found in You.

I pray that they would actively prepare themselves to share the gospel with others. May Your great commission become my children's mission in life. I pray that one day in heaven they will meet those who came to faith in You through their influence.

Amen.

Self-Centered

It is more blessed to give than to receive.

ACTS 20:35

Our Provider,

Everything we have comes from You. You are so gracious and lavish in the way You treat Your children. It is our desire to be like You.

I pray that my children would be faithful in stewarding all You give them. In every opportunity to care for those around them, may they be unselfish and generous. I ask that their lives would be rich with the blessings that come to those who give freely to others.

May they live with eyes that are always on the lookout for opportunities to give.

Amen.

Education

*Teach a youth about the way he should go;
even when he is old he will not depart from it.*

PROVERBS 22:6

God of All Knowledge and Wisdom,

I pray that You would give my children the hearts and spirits of lifelong learners. Would You put within them a desire to acquire new information and gain wisdom from it?

In science classes, may they see the wonder of Your creation in all things great and small. May they continually encounter You as the Great Designer and Sustainer of all things. In math classes, may they appreciate You as the God of logic, order, and completeness. In social studies, may they value You as the One who endowed the nations and people of this planet with such astounding diversity.

In history, may they see Your hand in the stories of individuals and nations and gain confidence in knowing that You not only raise them up but judge them in Your perfect time as well. Whenever they read and write, may they fall in love with the power of words and how they can be used to communicate life, hope, truth, joy, and encouragement to others.

May they experience Your presence and know You better through all their academic disciplines.

Amen.

Discernment

You must not bring any abhorrent thing into your house,
or you will be set apart for destruction like it.
You are to utterly detest and abhor it,
because it is set apart for destruction.

DEUTERONOMY 7:26

Our Fortress,

Most families struggle to determine which media influences they should and shouldn't allow in their homes. I need Your guidance to help our family make wise decisions regarding the influences that will affect my children in a negative way. Please lead me.

Lord, I also pray about the books, movies, games, music, and clothes my children will bring into our home. Please discourage them from engaging with anything impure or dishonoring to You. If they do, Father, please give me discernment in discussing these things with my children. I pray that You would lead our family into a grace-filled time of teaching and that my children would respond with tender, compliant spirits. May they also desire for the offensive items to be removed. Please help them avoid developing a taste for worldly things in their media choices.

May our entire family declare that we will set no evil thing before our eyes.

Amen.

Conceit

We must not become conceited, provoking
one another, envying one another.

GALATIANS 5:26

Mighty King,

I often ask You for good things in my children's future—rich blessings, fruitfulness, and success. I am aware that each success, whether academic, athletic, artistic, or spiritual, provides the enemy with an opportunity to slip in and tempt my children with pride.

I pray that my children would not give in to the temptation to be conceited or prideful. May they instead, in gratitude, bless You as the Giver of every good thing that comes their way.

I ask that You would give them humble spirits that are beautiful and attractive to others. May You be glorified not only in their successes but also in the praise they give You for their successes.

Amen.

Complaining

Do everything without grumbling and arguing.

PHILIPPIANS 2:14

Our Provider,

We live in a land and a time that, regardless of social class, places us among the most resourced and blessed people in the history of humankind. And yet we are arguably among the most discontented people as well.

I pray this would not be true of my children. May they realize that whatever their lot or status is in life (professionally, financially, or socially), You have allowed it and can bless them through it. May my children refuse to harbor a critical or ungrateful spirit but trust in Your will and provision for them.

May their faith in You keep them from grumbling and complaining.

Amen.

Generosity

A generous person will be blessed,
for he shares his food with the poor.

PROVERBS 22:9

God Who Gave Us His Best,

Many people go through each day looking for what can benefit them. Their eyes are set on what they can get out of life. I pray that my children would focus instead on what they can give to others.

May they seek out opportunities to be a blessing to others every day, whether that be through a kind word or some deed that meets a real need.

I fully trust that if my children seek to generously bless others, You will richly bless them in return.

Amen.

Unity

How good and pleasant it is
when brothers live together in harmony!

PSALM 133:1

God of Truth and Peace,

On a physical and relational level, I pray for unity between my children. As siblings, may they respect, love, and truly care for one another, and may it result in a sweet and peaceful life for all.

I pray that my children would also find like-hearted and like-minded friends. May they develop tight and caring bonds of faithfulness.

On a spiritual level, I ask that throughout my children's lives, Your Spirit would guide them into relationships with other believers who will be their brothers and sisters in the faith. I pray that these relationships would be built on a deep love for You and Your Word. May the beauty and peace of these relationships be examples to others of the blessing that comes when You are the center of a friendship.

Amen.

Goodness

The fruit of the Spirit is . . . goodness.

GALATIANS 5:22

Good Shepherd,

Often these days, it seems that referring to someone as "good" is almost like describing them with a term of derision or a put-down. Goodness is often simply not a quality that people celebrate.

Lord, I desire that my children would care deeply about all that is morally and spiritually excellent. May they value things of quality and the highest standards. And may their goodness reflect the beauty of Your character.

I ask that Your goodness would follow my children all the days of their lives.

Amen.

Procrastination

I hurried and did not delay
To keep Your commandments.

PSALM 119:60, NASB

God Who Does All He Says He Will Do,

I pray that my children would reflect Your character in their diligence. So many people are filled with good intentions but never seem to get around to doing what they say they will do. Would You teach my children the wisdom of doing quickly what they set out to do? May they experience the blessings that come from living this way.

Especially in relation to serving You, may they not delay in obeying the instructions they find in Your Word. As Your Spirit prompts their hearts, may they move immediately to carry out what You ask them to do.

I ask that my children would never be regarded as procrastinators but would honor You by following through on their commitments.

Amen.

Compassion

All of you should be like-minded and sympathetic,
should love believers, and be compassionate and humble.

1 PETER 3:8

God of Compassion,

You've been so lavish in the mercy You have shown us. You saw us as poor and needy and responded with what we needed most—a Savior.

I pray that my children would have tender and compassionate hearts toward others. May they identify with the lost and the least in the world. May they be moved to respond in a sweet, humble manner to those around them, showing love just as You would.

Please guard this tender place within them. Even if people should take advantage of their kindness, would You keep them from becoming cynical and hard-hearted? As Your hands in this world, may they continue to reach out with compassion.

Amen.

Responsibility

So then, each of us will give
an account of himself to God.

ROMANS 14:12

Our Foundation,

As my children come to understand Your Word, may they become aware of the reality that one day all people will stand before You to give an account of their lives. On this day, You will not judge or punish the sins of those who trust in Jesus (that was settled at the Cross) but will instead evaluate the quality of their work on earth.

I pray that my children would desire to do excellent work that brings You honor. May their conduct in this world, as well as their service to You, glorify Your name. Would You guide them in faithfully using the spiritual gifts You have given them?

May they build on Your foundation with gold and silver, not hay and straw. I ask that the fruit of their lives and labor would stand strong through the fire of Your inspection.

Amen.

Nearness of God

Remember, I am with you always,
to the end of the age.

MATTHEW 28:20

Our Ever-Present Help,

I can entrust my children to Your care because You, the All-Powerful One, will always be as close as their next breath. Whatever they face in life, may this truth be a great source of comfort to them.

In seasons when my children are dealing with loneliness or are feeling abandoned by a friend, may they turn to You and be strengthened by Your faithful presence.

In moments when my children feel fearful, please remind them that You are with them and will never leave them. May they find peace in knowing that You are always near.

Amen.

School

I am teaching you the way of wisdom;
I am guiding you on straight paths.

PROVERBS 4:11

Our Great Teacher,

Throughout childhood and their teenage years, my children will spend countless hours in educational settings preparing for what You have planned for them to do. In these settings, they will be exposed to a variety of people with different backgrounds, beliefs, and priorities.

During these years, I pray that You will

- use the influence of their instructors to help them grow in knowledge and wisdom;
- guard them from ungodly ideas and influences;
- ground them in Your truth and help them articulate their beliefs clearly; and
- keep them safe as they grow in mind, body, and spirit.

Amen.

Brevity of Life

LORD, reveal to me the end of my life
and the number of my days.
Let me know how short-lived I am.

PSALM 39:4

Eternal One,

Our days on this earth are brief in light of eternity. I pray that as Your Word of truth is poured into my children, they would reach the wise assessment that life is fleeting.

May this perspective make my children passionate and motivated to live every moment for You. May they not be prone to waste time but give themselves wholeheartedly to the work You have given them to do.

Would You lead them to live Kingdom-minded lives and help them make wise choices about how they spend their time?

May they take advantage of every opportunity to demonstrate Your love to others.

Amen.

Pressure

We are pressured in every way but not crushed;
we are perplexed but not in despair; we are persecuted
but not abandoned; we are struck down but not destroyed.

2 CORINTHIANS 4:8-9

Almighty One,

My children will be subject to many frustrations throughout their lives. Often these will come because of their limitations and weaknesses. But this is part of Your perfect design. You move and work through frail and faulty people as a testimony to the nations of Your great power.

I pray that my children would have firm confidence in Your ability to see them through the stresses and difficulties they face. May they know with certainty that they can endure anything by Your power. Would You remind them that they are never alone in the trials and pressures of life? May they always sense Your close companionship and experience the peace and hope that You alone are able to give.

In all their trials, and even their humiliations, may they find that weaknesses are opportunities for Your sustaining power to shine before the world.

Amen.

Peer Pressure

You must not follow a crowd in wrongdoing.

EXODUS 23:2

Savior and Lord,

Every child feels the temptation to follow others in doing wrong. We've all experienced the fear that washes over us when we consider whether to stand alone and oppose what the crowd is doing.

I pray that my children would develop at a young age the strength of character to stand on their own in doing what is right.

May their willingness to stand alone inspire others to resist evil as well, even when "everybody else is doing it."

Amen.

False Teaching

Don't be led astray by various kinds of strange teachings.

HEBREWS 13:9

God of All Truth,

The desire behind so many of my prayers is for my children to be deeply rooted in Your powerful and holy Word. I know that throughout their lives, my kids will encounter strange and heretical spiritual teachings. Some may even come from popular teachers. Others may come from those who once seemed biblical and orthodox.

May my children know the truth so well that they are able to discern what is false whenever it comes along. I pray that they would always consult Your Word to see what You have to say whenever they face suspicious teaching.

May their love of truth bear much fruit that honors You.

Amen.

Jealousy

A tranquil heart is life to the body,
but jealousy is rottenness to the bones.

PROVERBS 14:30

Provider of All We Need,

I believe that through every season of life, You will be faithful to provide all my children need. Please lead them to believe this truth and to be content with whatever You provide. May they be quick to remove the seeds of discontent that fall on the soil of their souls before they can bloom into full jealousy. I pray they would be so satisfied in their relationship with You that jealousy is unable to take root.

In today's verse, Lord, I see the relationship between the condition of our hearts and our outward behaviors. I ask that my children would pursue wisdom, purity, and holiness, and that this would be reflected in a healthy quality of life and a strong mind and body.

Amen.

Desires

Take delight in the LORD,
and He will give you your heart's desires.

PSALM 37:4

Our Light and Our Guide,

I come before You today asking that You would guide my children to wholeheartedly delight in You. May they find their life, their joy, their hope, and their purpose in You. Would You be the center and focus of their lives, as well as their great consuming passion?

As they delight in You, You have said that You will give them desires that are good, right, and holy. I pray that as my children look ahead to their future, they would feel free to pursue the desires You have placed in their hearts.

May they find life to be a joyous adventure as they pursue their dreams.

Amen.

Bullies

Love your enemies and pray for
those who persecute you.

MATTHEW 5:44

God of Grace,

Because of the broken world we live in, some people, for whatever reason, will seek to harm my children.

I pray that my children would have such faith in You as the ultimate, perfect Judge that they would freely leave the judgment of their enemies up to You. May they simply concern themselves with obeying Your command to love all people, even those who hate them.

Would You bring to my children's minds the spiritual state of those who persecute them? May they choose to pray for their enemies, asking You to lead their persecutors to repent of their wrong deeds and seek reconciliation with You and with them.

Amen.

Sorrow

The LORD gives, and the LORD takes away.
Praise the name of Yahweh.

JOB 1:21

God over All,

There will be times when life breaks my children's hearts, and watching that happen will break mine. Like all of us, my children will sometimes experience deep sorrow and loss.

In those times, may they find comfort in Your nearness and the presence of godly friends. I pray that my children would trust in Your sovereignty, believing that You love them and are working all things for good in their lives, even in those crushing moments.

May they trust You even though it is hard. May they worship You through their tears. Would You help them believe that You allow loss for a reason, and that even in the midst of it, You are good and wise? Give them the grace and strength to rise up, though filled with sadness, and still bless Your name.

Amen.

Loneliness

I will never leave you or forsake you.

HEBREWS 13:5

Our Constant Companion,

There will be moments in life when my children will feel the pangs of loneliness. They may feel this way when friends desert them or when they are simply learning how to handle a few hours of solitude.

In either case, may they find great comfort in Your promise to never leave or forsake them. Would You give them the certain assurance of Your nearness in these moments?

I ask that Your constant presence would strengthen and empower my children to press on through these trying times.

Amen.

Service

So if I, your Lord and Teacher, have washed your feet, you also ought to wash one another's feet.

JOHN 13:14

Our Loving Example,

Most of the prayers I pray for my children express a desire that their lives would bring them blessing and bring You honor. Reflecting Your love to this world is the best way to ensure this. Your Word helps us see that the essence of true love is self-sacrifice.

I ask that You would give my children attitudes of humility and service. Would You prompt them to look around for opportunities to meet real needs, just as You did? May they strive to put the interests of others ahead of their own. Always for Your glory, Lord.

Amen.

Character of God: Mystery

Just as you don't know the path of the wind,
or how bones develop in the womb of a pregnant woman,
so you don't know the work of God who makes everything.

ECCLESIASTES 11:5

Incomprehensible One,

You are so far above our understanding that we find ourselves in awe of You. I pray that You would reveal mysteries to my children, whether in Your Word, in a sermon, or in books about You, that would leave them overwhelmed and even speechless. May they frequently pause to ponder how inconceivable You are to the finite human mind. May they be lost in divine, holy wonder as they adore You.

Would You lead them to consider Your vastness, Your infinitude, and Your all-sufficiency? May it humble them to realize that even if they spend a lifetime studying You, they will simply scratch the surface of Your inexhaustible truth and love. Fill them with the awe of knowing You as a tender Father, even as they consider that many will know You only as a consuming fire.

May the unfathomable mystery of who You are lead them to great reverence, humility, and trust.

Amen.

Words

*I tell you that on the day of judgment
people will have to account for every careless word
they speak. For by your words you will be acquitted,
and by your words you will be condemned.*

MATTHEW 12:36-37

God of All Purity and Wisdom,

I come into Your presence today asking that my children would recognize the weight of their words. May they see that words are like stones they can throw at others to cause incredible damage or use to bring healing and build others up.

I pray that You would impress upon my children the responsibility of using their words wisely because their speech is a reflection of their spiritual state.

Please steer them away from deceitful, destructive, foolish, proud, or vulgar words. May they strive instead to always speak the truth in love, as You have called them to do.

Amen.

Decisions

Finalize plans with counsel.

PROVERBS 20:18

Light for Our Journey,

I come today, Lord, interceding on behalf of my children regarding the big decisions they will have to make in life. As they approach the second half of their teenage years, choices regarding college and work will loom large. They will face decisions about deepening relationships with members of the opposite sex. They will wrestle with discerning Your will and Your call on their lives.

In these important matters and so many others, I pray that they would seek out and listen to wise counsel. May their hearts be set on finding out not what is simply good but what is better and even best.

Will You consistently meet them through Your Word and through the wise counsel of godly leaders and friends?

Amen.

Love of Country

If . . . My people who are called by My name
humble themselves, pray and seek My face, and
turn from their evil ways, then I will hear from
heaven, forgive their sin, and heal their land.

2 CHRONICLES 7:13-14

Giver of Grace,

I pray that as my children grow, they would care deeply about the spiritual condition of our nation.

May they pray for political leaders, as You call them to do. Would You enable them to view our freedoms and liberties as opportunities to physically and spiritually bless others?

As they see policies, leaders, and agendas bring dishonor to You, would You lead my children to pray for revival in this nation and in the hearts of its people? May they be moved to intercede for all who live here, knowing that the only real hope for any of us comes through humility, prayer, repentance, and a longing for You.

Amen.

Assurance

I know the One I have believed in
and am persuaded that He is able to guard
what has been entrusted to me until that day.

2 TIMOTHY 1:12

Faithful God,

People, circumstances, and events will disappoint my children. People will make and break promises. "Love" will turn out to be temporary and conditional.

However, when it comes to You, may the truthfulness of Your promises and the unchanging nature of Your love give my children great assurance. May they never doubt Your promises or Your deep and abiding love for them.

Give them such confidence in who You are and the reality of Your coming Kingdom that they will live with a holy boldness through the power of Your Spirit.

Amen.

Heavenly-Minded

Set your minds on what is above,
not on what is on the earth.

COLOSSIANS 3:2

Lord of Heaven and Earth,

I pray that my children would come to understand that through saving faith in Your Son, they are indeed citizens of heaven. Even though their feet are firmly planted on earth, may their minds and thoughts be set on Your Kingdom.

May the tension of being *in* the world but not *of* the world lead them to look at everything in life through the lens of eternity. Would You guide them to make wise decisions after considering Your eternal perspective? May they value the things of heaven more than the things of earth.

Amen.

Temper

Patience is better than power,
and controlling one's temper, than capturing a city.

PROVERBS 16:32

Giver of Self-Control,

I pray that my children would see the incredible blessing that comes to those who control their tempers. Please teach them that true self-control is the fruit of walking in Your Spirit and allowing You to live through them. May they view self-control as a virtue of far greater value than any worldly success.

Even when they feel frustrated about not getting what they want, may they exercise patience and trust in You.

I understand that I will have much more influence in my children's lives by modeling this virtue rather than merely talking about it. Lord, please help me set an example for them as one who restrains any anger and frustration I feel.

Amen.

Sadness

Be gracious to me, LORD,
because I am in distress;
my eyes are worn out from angry sorrow—
my whole being as well.

PSALM 31:9

Comforter,

I pray that my children would know You as the source of their greatest joys in life. May they see Your good hand behind every blessing that comes their way.

May they come to know You even more intimately in times of sadness and sorrow. On days when they feel alone, disappointed, upset, or rejected, be gracious to them and help them draw near to You. I pray that they would know You as the Faithful One who never disappoints. May they always find comfort in Your loving presence.

Would You use sadness and distress to draw them close to You?

Amen.

Character

Do not be deceived:
"Bad company corrupts good morals."

1 CORINTHIANS 15:33

Wise and Faithful Friend,

At times, I prefer that my children not spend so much time with some of their peers. I can't control which people my children will be exposed to, but You, Lord, can control which friendships develop. Please bring friends of good character and morals into their lives.

I pray that my children would be drawn to peers with common values. May my children simply refuse to let those who are bad influences speak into their lives.

May Your Holy Spirit draw near and give them wisdom in choosing their friends. I ask that they would avoid bad company and seek out good company instead.

Amen.

Spiritual Growth

*Solid food is for the mature—for those whose senses
have been trained to distinguish between good and evil.*

HEBREWS 5:14

Our Master and Teacher,

Just as I hope to see my children grow physically and mentally,
I also desire to see them mature spiritually. I especially pray that
they would be drawn to Your Word.

May my children not simply hear Your truth but willingly put
into practice all that You command them to do.

Give them an attraction to the deeper truths of Your Word. At
the appropriate time, as my children outgrow the milk of elementary teaching, may they acquire a taste for the meat of doctrine
and theology. I ask that this would not lead to pride but to greater
fruitfulness for Your glory.

Amen.

Mentors

*We cared so much for you that we were pleased to
share with you not only the gospel of God but also our
own lives, because you had become dear to us.*

1 THESSALONIANS 2:8

Shepherd of the Saints,

I will strive to teach, train, and prepare my children for what
lies ahead. However, I know I can do only so much. What You have
for them to do will require the influence of others with more specific skill sets than I possess.

I pray that my children's lives would be rich with mentors along
the way. Will You bless my kids with coaches, teachers, professors,
pastors, and supervisors who see their potential and take the initiative to invest in them?

May all these mentors be worthy of my children's respect and
emulation. I ask that they would not just sharpen my children with
academic and professional skills but would also show them how to
live with faith and integrity.

Amen.

Parenting: Guidance

Everyone must be quick to hear,
slow to speak, and slow to anger.

JAMES 1:19

Perfect Father,

I have prayed about this verse being true in the lives of my children. I come today asking that it would also be true in my life as I interact with my children.

A normal day can be filled with stress, interruptions, and too much to get done. I confess that when I am tired and stretched to the limit, I can be short-tempered with my children.

God, please give me wisdom and patience to listen well to my children—not to interrupt but to really pay attention and communicate that they are worthy of my time and undistracted focus.

Please guide me in being slow to speak and slow to get angry. I know this is possible only as Your Spirit fills and leads me. Thank You that You always desire to hear Your children speak. I want to be like You. I need You today and every day.

Amen.

Inadequacies

*"There's a boy here who has five barley loaves
and two fish." . . . Jesus took the loaves, and after giving
thanks He distributed them to those who were seated—
so also with the fish, as much as they wanted.*

JOHN 6:9, 11

Miracle Worker,

You can perform any work or wonder You desire simply through Your own power. And yet so often we see that You choose to work through imperfect and inadequate people.

I know that my children, like everyone else, will be painfully aware of their inadequacies. Whenever this happens, may they recall the young boy from today's passage and choose to focus on Your sufficiency.

I pray they would never forget that You are the God of might and miracles and that You can use whatever they offer You. Reassure them that they are not too young (nor too old), too limited, or too short of knowledge or skill. I ask that they would instead offer You all they are and all they have and then stand back in awe of what You can help them accomplish.

Amen.

Thought Life

May the words of my mouth
and the meditation of my heart
be acceptable to You,
LORD, my rock and my Redeemer.

PSALM 19:14

Holy One,

I pray that today's verse would be true in my own life and in the lives of my children.

You know the meditations of our hearts, Lord. Nothing is ever hidden from Your sight. Before we even speak, our words are birthed from some thought or belief within us. Streams of pure and impure thoughts flow into our hearts and become deep pools.

May we filter out whatever is impure in our hearts and our speech so that only what is pure and holy remains. Guide us, Lord, so that every thought and word would be a pleasing and acceptable offering to You.

Amen.

Choices

*It is a sin for the person who knows to do
what is good and doesn't do it.*

JAMES 4:17

Shepherd of Our Souls,

Through Your Word and Your Spirit, You reveal our acts of rebellion that defy Your expressed will and are sin against You. I pray that this kind of disobedience would be rare in the lives of my children.

At other times, You reveal things we should be doing but are neglecting. Like all of us, my children will sometimes be tempted to be passive and negligent in their walk with You.

I pray that they would reject passivity, as well as a rebellious spirit, and seek instead to obey what You have called them to do. May their hearts always be tender to the promptings of Your Spirit, and may they choose to honor You through obedience.

Amen.

Critical Spirit

You, why do you criticize your brother? Or you, why do you look down on your brother? For we will all stand before the tribunal of God.

ROMANS 14:10

Righteous Judge,

You see and evaluate all things and all people perfectly. I pray that my children would embrace this truth and never feel the need to judge another person, especially another believer.

Sometimes other Christians will aggravate and frustrate my children or behave in ways that would seem to deny Your name. When this happens, may my children pray for them and—if given the opportunity—speak the truth in tender and compassionate love.

May my children never have harsh or self-righteous spirits.

Amen.

Prayer

This is the confidence we have before [God]: Whenever
we ask anything according to His will, He hears us.

1 JOHN 5:14

God Who Hears Us,

I ask that my children would desire regular, rich times of prayer with You. What freedom You have given us that we may ask for anything in Your name. Bless You!

I pray that my children's prayer times would not just be moments of making requests for what they want and need but would also be filled with worship, confession, and thanksgiving

As they present their requests to You, may they always pray as Your Son did in Gethsemane: "Not My will, but Yours, be done." More than things for themselves, may they want what You want for them.

Amen.

Strongholds

If anyone is in Christ, he is a new creation;
old things have passed away, and look, new things have come.

2 CORINTHIANS 5:17

God Who Gives Freedom,

Every family passes down from generation to generation some wonderful qualities and traits. Every family also shares some areas of weaknesses and struggle.

Lord, I ask that any propensities toward sin I may have inherited through my family would be broken. I don't even know them all, but You do. I repent of them and ask for Your cleansing and strength to overcome their influence over my life.

You are almighty God, greater than any force or device the enemy might use against us. Would You give my children freedom from generational strongholds?

Amen.

Priorities

The one who pursues righteousness and faithful love
will find life, righteousness, and honor.

PROVERBS 21:21

Righteous God,

I ask that my children would pursue righteousness in their relationships. First and foremost, may they always strive to be in a right relationship with You. I pray they would be quick to confess their sins and do what pleases You.

Then may they examine their closest relationships to see if all is well. Make them aware of any unresolved offenses and prompt them to seek reconciliation.

As they pursue the priorities that matter to You, may they enjoy a rich overflow of Your blessings in their lives.

Amen.

Gossip

Without wood, fire goes out;
without a gossip, conflict dies down.

PROVERBS 26:20

God Who Is Truth and Loves Truth,

We all know how it feels to not only pass along gossip but also be the target of other people's gossip. We know this destructive habit has no place in the lives of Your followers.

May my children reject the petty game of tearing down someone else to build themselves up. I pray that they would choose, even from a young age, to not engage in activities that promote slander, strife, or dissent.

May they instead seek to be peacemakers in the midst of conflict.

Amen.

Future

*We are His creation, created in Christ Jesus
for good works, which God prepared ahead
of time so that we should walk in them.*

EPHESIANS 2:10

Master Designer,

With great joy and anticipation, I think about my children's future. You have uniquely gifted and wired them for paths of service You had in mind for them from before the foundation of the world. How wild! How wonderful!

Watching the paths their lives take will be like watching a beautiful flower slowly unfold. Day by day and step by step, Your plans and purposes will reveal themselves.

I pray that my children's good works would richly bless and glorify You. Praise You for their perfect design!

Amen.

Friends with Nonbelievers

Act wisely toward outsiders,
making the most of the time.

COLOSSIANS 4:5

God Who Is Light,

Sometime at a young age, my children will begin to spend time around nonbelievers. It may be at school, in the neighborhood, or through sports and other activities, but they will eventually realize that some people have different values and beliefs from those of our family.

I pray that as they grow, my children would be more aware of their responsibility to be light in the darkness.

May they act with authentic love and concern toward unbelievers. I pray they would be wise in their behavior and worthy of respect as they take advantage of opportunities they have to speak truth and life. May all they do be for the glory of the gospel.

Amen.

Joy

Our mouths were filled with laughter then,
and our tongues with shouts of joy.
Then they said among the nations,
"The LORD has done great things for them."

PSALM 126:2

Our Dwelling Place,

As You reside with us in our home, I ask that joy would abound. Would You create an environment where my children would grow up enjoying fellowship with one another and their friends?

May all who enter our home feel welcome and valued. I also pray that You would foster a spirit of ease through shared laughter and that these walls would resound with music that honors You.

Be near us, Lord Jesus.

Amen.

Future Spouse

Do not be mismatched with unbelievers.
For what partnership is there between
righteousness and lawlessness? Or what
fellowship does light have with darkness?

2 CORINTHIANS 6:14

Holy One,

I ask many things of You regarding my children's potential spouses—that they would be loving, faithful, forgiving, and respectful. But most of all, I ask that they would passionately love You first and foremost. May their faith clearly be the most important part of their lives. I also pray that their love for You, Your Word, and Your people would be evident.

Along the way, would You keep my children from entering into romantic or dating relationships with someone who is not a Christian? I even ask that they would not be interested in someone of the opposite sex whose faith is new, young, or immature.

Wherever their future spouses are today, Lord, please surround, protect, and bless them.

Amen.

Discernment

*I am Your servant; give me understanding
so that I may know Your decrees.*

PSALM 119:125

Word of God,

Would You bless my children with good Bible teachers from their childhood classes at church, through high school youth ministry, and even in college-age groups? May those who lead them handle Your Word with understanding and integrity. Ground my children in Your truth, Father, and give them discerning hearts.

I pray that You would feed my children's love for Your Word and equip them to discern truth from lies in conversations and in the culture.

Amen.

Money

Your life should be free from the love of money.
Be satisfied with what you have.

HEBREWS 13:5

God of an Everlasting Kingdom,

Today I lift up to You my children's dreams for the future. Whatever career paths they choose, I pray that my children would not be driven simply by a desire for financial gain. Instead, may they passionately desire to live for You.

I ask that they would look at this great world of need, consider how You've gifted them, and seek out careers where they can best use their gifts for Your glory. As they serve You, would You take care of them and provide for every need?

May their hearts be free from the love and pursuit of material possessions.

Amen.

Kindness

The fruit of the Spirit is . . . kindness.

GALATIANS 5:22

Merciful One,

Instill in my children the strength and compassion they need to lead lives of kindness. May they show tender concern for friends and family daily.

In moments when they are tempted to react in anger or frustration, may they instead choose a kind and gentle response.

Would You faithfully convict them when they are more concerned about themselves than others? May they turn from their selfishness and pursue kindness. I pray that they would discover at an early age the blessing and joy that awaits those who treat others with compassion.

Amen.

Correction

No discipline seems enjoyable at the time, but painful.
Later on, however, it yields the fruit of peace and
righteousness to those who have been trained by it.

HEBREWS 12:11

Wise Shepherd,

You have certainly used unpleasant circumstances to change my heart in ways that pleased You and produced fruit in my life. Throughout my children's lives, they will face times of discipline and correction from Your hand, from their parents, and even from teachers, coaches, or bosses.

Would You give my children tender hearts and teachable spirits?

I pray that the difficulties and pain of being corrected would lead to greater wisdom and righteousness in their lives. May they find peace in knowing that You and their parents will always guide them with hearts of love.

Amen.

Parenting: Confession

Confess your sins to one another.

JAMES 5:16

Restorer of Unity,

Today I am mindful that as my children grow, there will be times when I wrong them. This is far from my heart's desire, but it will happen. In a moment of stress or anger, my words may be careless or hurtful. On some occasions, I may misjudge a situation and make a wrong decision that causes my children distress or harm.

In those moments, may I be quick to apologize to my children and ask for their forgiveness, and may they be quick to forgive.

Because You are our beautiful Redeemer, will You use even these hard times to capture my children's hearts with the beauty of humility, confession, grace, and unity?

Amen.

Worship

Ascribe to Yahweh the glory due His name.

PSALM 29:2

Worthy One,

I pray that from a young age my children would love to worship You. I'm not asking that they would simply enjoy the music and emotions that are stirred up in corporate gatherings, but rather that they would find delight in exalting You for being the one true God. May their hearts be consumed by the glory, goodness, and wonder of You.

Would You move them to worship You not only when they gather with other believers but in times of solitude as well?

May they worship You in spirit—with the right heart attitude and passion—and in truth—in consistency with what Scripture teaches.

Let their worship always glorify Your name.

Amen.

Character of God: Wrath

God is a righteous judge
and a God who shows His wrath every day.

PSALM 7:11

Perfect Judge,

Your wrath is an attribute we don't often think about. Yet it is another expression of Your perfect nature. You express Your perfect fury toward any offense against Your holiness. Disregarding sin or showing indifference toward it would be a less-than-perfect response on Your part.

I pray that as my children get older and begin to grasp even just the crumbs of this great truth regarding Your holiness, may they be filled with gratitude for Your salvation that delivered them from Your wrath.

May this truth also lead my children to love what You love and to hate what You hate. I pray that it would spur them on to greater holiness for Your glory.

Amen.

Joy

Weeping may spend the night,
but there is joy in the morning.

PSALM 30:5

God of Every New Dawn,

My children will go through difficult times—times of sadness and loss, periods of testing and trial, seasons of waiting and uncertainty—all normal dark nights of the soul.

In these times, may they keep their eyes fixed on You—trusting You, seeking You, praising You. May they find that in Your perfect time, these nights always end. And for those who trust You, joy isn't based on circumstances. We can experience joy even in the midst of trials.

Even when they find themselves sitting in shadows, may my children never lose their hope and anticipation of seeing the light of a new day.

Amen.

Appearance

Man does not see what the LORD sees,
for man sees what is visible,
but the LORD sees the heart.

1 SAMUEL 16:7

God Who Made Us and Knows Us,

Today's passage seems radically countercultural. We live in a world that is totally obsessed with appearance. This ever-present fixation, especially from media in all its forms, is an incredibly destructive force in the lives of so many children and young adults.

I pray that my children would instead value what You value. May they invest more care and attention in cultivating inner beauty—their character, integrity, purity, and spiritual lives.

May they also assess other people on inner qualities of virtue and integrity rather than on outward physical qualities.

Amen.

Grudges

Don't say, "I will avenge this evil!"
Wait on the LORD, and He will rescue you.

PROVERBS 20:22

Our Defender,

Your care for Your children is evident throughout our lives. Physically and spiritually, You perfectly provide all we need. You are also our Shield and Deliverer when others treat us unjustly.

In this fallen world, my children will be offended or wronged at times. Though they may feel hurt or abandoned, may they also feel that You are near and You understand their pain.

May they trust that You will deal perfectly with those who wrong them. I pray that they would be able to forgive and let go of the hurt instead of seeking revenge. May they find comfort in knowing that You will take care of Your children in the end and that the time and manner of Your justice are completely up to You.

Amen.

Freedom from Fear

*I sought the LORD, and He answered me
and delivered me from all my fears.*

PSALM 34:4

Our Refuge,

Throughout their lives, my children will encounter things that frighten them—nightmares, strangers, and near accidents, as well as challenging and unusual situations.

May they learn at an early age to call on You in those times. Though fear may grip them, it cannot hold them in its power forever. As they cry out to You for help, let them see that Your power is greater than any other.

Build their faith as they seek You each time they're afraid. May they experience You as the God who delivers them from all their fears.

Amen.

Laziness

A slacker's craving will kill him
because his hands refuse to work.

PROVERBS 21:25

Righteous Father,

Lazy children are a grief to You, as well as to their earthly parents. You are diligent, and you delight in hard work. You work perfectly in all things for Your glory and our benefit.

Heavenly Father, turn my children away from laziness. May they be diligent in housework, schoolwork, and any jobs they take on.

If they struggle with a bent toward laziness, please guide my words and help me instruct them carefully and wisely.

Ultimately, no matter what I say, only You can change a heart. If my children reject my instruction and persist in laziness, will You do whatever You must to turn them away from foolishness and toward wisdom?

Amen.

Integrity

The one who lives with integrity lives securely,
but whoever perverts his ways will be found out.

PROVERBS 10:9

God Who Sees and Knows All,

I pray that my children would live with clear consciences because You have shaped their character.

When they sin against You or offend others, may they be quick to repent and make things right. Would You give them confidence in knowing that You forgive whatever they confess?

May the ways they go about their daily lives be consistent with what they profess. Help them walk in integrity for all their days so that their lives would bring glory to You.

Amen.

Perseverance

Do not become sluggish, but imitate those who through faith and patience inherit the promises.

HEBREWS 6:12, NKJV

Great God,

You are the God of intentionality and diligence. Before the creation of the world, You set Your great plan of redemption in motion, and You will persevere in bringing it to completion.

I pray that as my children make plans, large and small, they would follow through with what they begin. May they not give up when they face setbacks or discouragement. I know that weariness and exhaustion will set in, but please help them look to You as the One who renews their strength.

Would You provide the endurance and perseverance they need to finish the work they take on?

Amen.

Pride

As it is, you boast in your arrogance.
All such boasting is evil.

JAMES 4:16

Mighty Yet Meek Savior,

Pride is the seedbed for many sins that sprout from human hearts. To avoid the sins that disrupt and destroy relationships, I pray that my children would desire and maintain humble spirits.

If their pride goes unchecked, they could lose inner joy, peace, and confidence. They could also lose their desire for drawing near to You in worship and adoration.

Instead, may they stay in a right relationship with You. In humility, may they be loving, gracious, and helpful as they relate to others.

Amen.

God's Word

Happy is the man who fears the L ORD*,*
taking great delight in His commands.

PSALM 112:1

Living God,

Every good parent desires lives of blessing for their children.

Your Word is clear that the key to a life of blessing is reverence for You and loving obedience to Your Word. God, I ask that my children would eagerly desire and reflect these qualities. May they esteem You as the Most High and Holy God, and may Your Word be their delight. I pray that obedience would be their first response to Your Word.

May You bless them with lives of joy, hope, and peace that come to all who delight in You.

Amen.

Faith

*Everyone who will acknowledge Me before men, I will
also acknowledge him before My Father in heaven.*

MATTHEW 10:32

Lord,

I pray that my children would be bold in their faith. From the moment they trust in You, may they not hesitate to announce this decision to their family, friends, and church. May they also desire to follow You in baptism.

Would You lead my children to publicly acknowledge their faith often? I pray that their words as well as their actions would clearly proclaim that You are their Savior and Lord.

May they never deny You in word or deed, or even by their silence. If they should experience a lapse in faithfulness, I ask that they would be quick to confess their sin and receive Your forgiveness. When they do, would You bring them back to a clear and strong confession of their faith in You?

Amen.

Influence

No one should seek his own good, but the good of the
other person. . . . Whether you eat or drink, or whatever
you do, do everything for God's glory. Give no offense
to the Jews or the Greeks or the church of God.

1 CORINTHIANS 10:24, 31-32

God Who Gives Freedom,

As my children grow, may they be aware of the influence they have on others. May they guard the integrity of their witness and seek the good of others in every situation.

My children will face some things in life that are not explicitly forbidden in Your Word. As they wrestle with these issues, may they ask themselves whether such things are profitable and edifying.

May they care so much about Your glory that they would gladly set aside their freedom to avoid being a stumbling block to someone else.

Amen.

Confidence

*Let us approach the throne of grace
with boldness, so that we may receive mercy
and find grace to help us at the proper time.*

HEBREWS 4:16

Our Compassionate High Priest,

Your tenderness and kindness mean so much to us. You understand our weaknesses and struggles. You have felt what we feel. Bless You for Your grace and mercy.

When my children are struggling, I pray that they would find hope in Your compassionate invitation and boldly ask for Your help. May the fact that You long for them to draw near to You lead them to call out to You continually.

I pray that the certainty of finding grace and love in Your presence would give them confidence to approach Your throne.

Amen.

Mind

*Do not be conformed to this age, but be transformed
by the renewing of your mind, so that you may discern
what is the good, pleasing, and perfect will of God.*

ROMANS 12:2

Shepherd Who Leads Us into Purity,

I pray that my children would love You with all their minds. As an expression of that love, may they vigorously guard what they allow to enter their minds—what they watch, read, listen to, and talk about.

I ask that You would give them a passionate love for Your Word. May they saturate themselves with it, spending rich hours studying and meditating on Your truth.

Would You give my children sound minds? Please renew their minds daily and keep them from negativity and confusion. I also ask that You would protect them from mental illness.

Amen.

Purity

The pure in heart are blessed,
for they will see God.

MATTHEW 5:8

Holy One,

You have called Your people to be holy as You are holy. We desire to be holy, yet we are powerless to accomplish this without Your Spirit.

Just as heat purifies gold and removes contaminants, I pray that You would burn away any unfaithfulness in my children and give them pure hearts. May their devotion to You be undivided. I pray that they would be single-minded in their love and loyalty to You.

May they turn away from anything that would steal the attention and affection that should be Yours alone.

Amen.

Challenge to Faith

First, be aware of this:
Scoffers will come in the last days to scoff,
living according to their own desires.

2 PETER 3:3

Living God,

At some point along the way, my children will have their first encounter with someone in an academic setting who will challenge their faith. It may be in high school, college, or graduate school, but it will be a memorable experience that will mark their lives.

Regardless of how my children handle the encounter outwardly (whether they are able to articulate their faith in the moment), I care much more about how it will affect them inwardly. In the midst of this challenge, may they know the comforting presence, counsel, and encouragement of Your Spirit. May the experience push them to become more certain of what they believe and why. I ask this knowing that as they dig deeper, they will always find You to be true and faithful.

As our Redeemer, would You please use these difficult situations in the lives of my children to accomplish something that is beautiful, powerful, beneficial, and glorifying to You?

Amen.

Spiritual Power

*The One who is in you is greater than
the one who is in the world.*

1 JOHN 4:4

Almighty,

No power is like Your power. Ultimately, every human being, angel, and demon—even Satan himself—will bow before You and confess that Christ is Lord!

For now, we face an enemy who is real, powerful, and active in our world. May my children have full confidence in Your greater power. I pray that their faith would triumph over any fear that may rise within them.

As others in our culture foolishly celebrate themes and images of the kingdom of darkness, may these things hold no fear for my children. May every encounter simply remind them that no power in the universe compares to Yours. You are supreme and victorious!

Amen.

Friends

While Moses held up his hand, Israel prevailed,
but whenever he put his hand down, Amalek prevailed.
When Moses' hands grew heavy, they took a stone and
put it under him, and he sat down on it. Then Aaron
and Hur supported his hands, one on one side and
one on the other so that his hands remained
steady until the sun went down.

EXODUS 17:11-12

Faithful One,

Times will surely come when my children will need hope, encouragement, and the company of faithful, godly friends as they serve You. Would You guide them to friends who are not only true but will also build them up and lead them into Your blessings?

May my children know the sweet fellowship of like-hearted brothers and sisters. Would You bring them to a community of faith where, along with others, they can experience You doing great things?

I ask that You would help my children be friends who are a great encouragement to others. Please allow them to experience the joy of teamwork, for Your glory.

Amen.

Kindness

The Lord's bond-servant must not be quarrelsome,
but be kind to all.

2 TIMOTHY 2:24, NASB

Lamb of God,

These are days when meekness and kindness are not celebrated as virtues, and yet in Your Kingdom they are prized. I pray that in my children's lives, these qualities would be the beautiful fruit born from hearts of humility.

May my children see other people as Your creations and treat them with great respect. I pray that they would always exhibit spirits of tenderness and kindness.

When they find themselves in situations that require them to be forceful and bold, may they do so without ever being harsh, overbearing, or unkind.

Amen.

Repentance

Be gracious to me, God,
according to Your faithful love. . . .
Wash away my guilt
and cleanse me from my sin. . . .
Against You—You alone—I have sinned
and done this evil in Your sight.

PSALM 51:1-2, 4

Faithful Forgiver,

Would You give my children tender spirits toward You when it comes to their sin? May they realize that although they may have wronged or hurt someone else, it is ultimately You they have sinned against by failing to obey Your Word.

I pray that my children be would quick to confess their sins to You. May their cries of repentance be sincere, never just an appearance of sorrow without truly turning from sin and turning toward You. Soften their hearts and root out any stubbornness or obstinance when Your Spirit is convicting them.

When they cry out for mercy, may they know the sweet peace of Your acceptance and the deep joy of being restored to a right relationship with You.

Amen.

Obedience

This is love:
that we walk according to His commands.

2 JOHN 1:6

Lord,

Throughout Your Word, You make clear that being in a right relationship with You means taking You at Your word and doing whatever You are calling us to do. This truth remains constant: to love You and trust You is to obey You.

May my children's love for You be an active love, just as active as walking. May they quickly and willingly do the things You call them to do.

I ask that You would give my children a deep desire to know You more, and may that draw them daily to Your Word. May they believe that their simple and pure obedience greatly honors You.

Amen.

Salvation

*I am the way, the truth, and the life. No one
comes to the Father except through Me.*

JOHN 14:6

The Only Way,

My children will grow up in a world that insists there are many ways to come to God. Many people find the exclusivity of one way offensive. But You, our Savior, have the right to claim that You are the *only way* to God.

I pray that this would be a foundational and immovable plank in my children's theology. May they trust in You alone and clearly communicate this truth at every opportunity.

Would You impress upon them the wisdom of entering the narrow gate of salvation and walking the difficult road that leads to everlasting life? May they have a passion to share this truth with others.

Amen.

Confidence

I am sure of this, that He who started a good work in you will carry it on to completion until the day of Christ Jesus.

PHILIPPIANS 1:6

Faithful One,

As my children grow, they will reflect on life at times and find it random and incomplete. When they face uncertainties, difficulties, and even moments of defeat, they might feel as if they are wandering along without a clear aim or purpose.

I pray that today's verse will speak hope to them and give them confidence in Your faithfulness. May it draw them back to Your character and the assurance that those You call, You will also justify; and those You justify, You will also glorify.

Even today, Lord, would You speak peace to my own soul and remind me that my children are Yours and that You have great plans for them in this life and beyond?

Bless You, loving Father.

Amen.

Parenting: Conversations

*Teach [God's commands] to your children, talking about
them when you sit in your house and when you walk along
the road, when you lie down and when you get up. Write
them on the doorposts of your house and on your gates.*

DEUTERONOMY 11:19-20

God Who Is My God,

Your Word teaches me that my conversations with my children
in all the ordinary moments of life should be about You. I ask today
for Your wisdom and help to do this with diligence and excellence.

May I use every situation in life to point my children to You.
For this to happen, I need You to change me and open my eyes to
Your ever-present work around me. Guide me with wisdom from
Your Word that will be appropriate for conversations with my
children.

I want to take advantage of daily drive times, mealtimes, bed-
times, work-around-the-house times, hang-out times, and fun
times—every opportunity I have—to make much of You and remind
my children of Your greatness. May the days spent within the walls
of our home prepare my children for what You have in store for
them. Please help me make Your presence a part of every moment
of our home life.

Amen.

Identity

In [God] we live and move and exist.

ACTS 17:28

God Who Calls Us His Own,

It is only natural that as my children grow, they will ask themselves, *What is my true identity?* and consider what the world has to say. As they search for answers to this question, may they discover, first and foremost, that they are *children of God*.

The enemy wants to lead my children down dark alleyways of false identity. He will begin by trying to convince them that their failures and mistakes define them. May Your cross always tell them a different and truer story of who they are. I pray that they would hold to the truth that by Your grace, their moments of weakness do not define them.

The enemy might also try to connect my children with people who are committed to a certain sin, lifestyle, or false identity. Would You help my children quickly and clearly recognize that these groups or communities do not reflect Your values?

May my children live in confidence, now and forever, that they belong to You.

Amen.

Plans

Commit your activities to the LORD,
and your plans will be achieved.

PROVERBS 16:3

Giver of the Desires of Our Hearts,

It excites me when I think about the dreams and potential You have put within my children. What a thrill it will be watching these blossom and begin to unfold.

I pray that my children would always seek Your heart and Your desires for their lives. May they ask how You would like to use them and seek to follow Your steps along the path of life.

I also pray that they would hold their dreams in open hands and submit to Your will. It will be a joy to behold where their righteous plans will take them as You bless them and give them success.

Amen.

Ministry

How can they call on Him they have not believed in?
And how can they believe without hearing about
Him? And how can they hear without a preacher?
And how can they preach unless they are sent?

ROMANS 10:14-15

Head of the Church,

It's clear that all who call on You for salvation are not just to be saints but also to be ministers of the gospel. While we live and breathe, we serve You with our lives. We build up and encourage other believers and share the gospel with the lost.

Perhaps You will call my children to a church or parachurch ministry, or some other ministry position. If this is Your plan for them, I pray that this ministry would be a place where my children can use their gifts and talents to bring You glory.

If Your purpose for my children is a place of secular employment, I pray that they would see it as their mission field and minister each day to those with whom they come in contact.

May my children serve You wherever You call them to work.

Amen.

Veterans Day

No one has greater love than this, that someone would lay down his life for his friends.

JOHN 15:13

Our Defender and Sustainer,

I want my children to have a profound gratitude for all the courageous men and women who have bravely served in the armed forces to protect and preserve our great nation.

I pray that my children would respect, honor, and express thanks to service members whenever they have an opportunity.

May my children regard with the highest esteem those who have sacrificed selflessly to guard our freedom.

Amen.

Witness

You will be My witnesses in Jerusalem, in all Judea
and Samaria, and to the ends of the earth.

ACTS 1:8

Good News for All the World,

I pray that my children would seek out opportunities to witness for You. May they passionately desire others to know how You saved them, changed them, and gave them hope, joy, peace, and purpose.

In all the ways they communicate with others, may my children be quick to speak of Your power and Your goodness.

Guide them as they learn how to share the gospel with others and give witness to Your grace in their lives. May they desire with all their hearts that all people would come to know You.

Amen.

Faith

*Simon, Simon, look out! Satan has asked
to sift you like wheat. But I have prayed for you
that your faith may not fail. And you, when you
have turned back, strengthen your brothers.*

LUKE 22:31-32

Enduring One,

I know there will be times when You allow the enemy to test my children. They will be shaken or tempted or tried in some way that will reveal to what extent they are truly trusting in You. I am aware that, in various situations, my children will give in to temptations.

Though they may fail these tests, Lord, may their faith in You never fail. When they stumble, may they be quick to repent and seek an intimate relationship with You once again.

May their belief in You and their devotion to You be proved genuine, unfailing, and enduring.

Amen.

Conviction

If your brother . . . or your closest friend secretly entices
you, saying, "Let us go and worship other gods," . . .
you must not yield to him or listen to him.

DEUTERONOMY 13:6, 8

Lord God,

I pray that as my children mature, they would become persons of deep conviction. May they be strong and confident in what they believe. I pray that not even the influence of close friends would shake or compromise their faith in You.

Would You give my children the courage and willingness to go against the flow of the culture and not be swayed by winds of false spiritual teaching? May they be so confident in who You are and the perfect authority of Your Word that they would always stand for what is good, pure, loving, and right.

Amen.

Character of God: Omnipresent

The highest heaven cannot contain [God].

2 CHRONICLES 2:6

The Ever-Present One,

You are everywhere all the time. Nothing will ever confine You. You are without limits of any kind. You reign over earth, heaven, and hell. You even enter the hearts of sinners to convict them of their sin. You are in every moment of the past, present, and future. You fill every inch of this universe and beyond.

I pray that these marvelous truths would be a great source of comfort and hope for my children. Would You assure them of Your nearness in each trial and temptation they face? May Your presence be a great strength for them when they are called to serve You in some challenging way.

I ask that Your omnipresence would motivate my children to be holy in their decisions and actions. May they realize that any moment of sin, whether in thought, word, or deed, is a moment lived out in Your presence.

Amen.

Strength

*I am able to do all things
through Him who strengthens me.*

PHILIPPIANS 4:13

Our Strength,

I pray that my children would have upbeat, positive spirits that flow from a deep faith and confidence in who You are. May they believe they can face anything life brings their way because of Your power in their lives.

Would You fill my children with courage to face trouble, pressure, temptation, and trials, knowing that they can overcome in Your strength?

Heavenly Father, Your great power is beyond anything we can imagine. I pray that my children experience that amazing power throughout their lives. May the knowledge that they can do all things through You give them hope-filled, can-do spirits.

Amen.

Diligence

Do not grow weary in doing good.

2 THESSALONIANS 3:13

The God Who Sees,

There will be times when my children will see people taking advantage of the government, the church, or other agencies designed to help those in need. We know how disheartening this can be, especially when we're diligently trying to do what is right.

When this happens, I ask that my children would trust that You will deal with offenders in Your perfect time. May my children not grow weary doing what is good and right and pleasing to You. When they're discouraged, would You remind them that You know all, see all, and always act justly?

May this bring them renewed encouragement and diligence.

Amen.

Stewardship of Talents

*Grace was given to each one of us according
to the measure of the Messiah's gift.*

EPHESIANS 4:7

Equipper of the Saints,

I trust that You have uniquely gifted my children to serve You and Your church. I pray that You would equip me to help my children develop their gifts and abilities. Would You show me where they might need special nurturing and where to find lessons or training that could cultivate their gifts?

I ask that, through Your Spirit, You would reveal to my children what their giftings are. Though my children will change over the years, may they always follow Your leading and be good stewards of the gifts You have given them.

Please guard their giftings from being used for lesser purposes than what You desire. May they always be used for Your glory.

Amen.

Work

It is also the gift of God whenever anyone eats,
drinks, and enjoys all his efforts.

ECCLESIASTES 3:13

One Who Gives Life Meaning,

I ask that You would direct my children to work that is meaningful to them and honoring to You.

Even from a young age, may they find enjoyment and deep satisfaction in various activities. Would You use these interests, along with wise and godly counsel from Your Word, to set my children on the life path You have planned for them? Even if they change jobs several times during their lives, may they move from one type of work that gives them joy to something that gives them even greater joy. May they be grateful for the work You provide and find satisfaction in doing it with excellence.

I pray that they would bless You for leading them into meaningful and purposeful labor.

Amen.

Persistence

We must not get tired of doing good, for we will
reap at the proper time if we don't give up.

GALATIANS 6:9

Persistent Faithful One,

You have ordained good works for all Your children to do. Some good works may be short-term, while others might continue for a lifetime. I pray that my children would be committed to completing all the tasks You've given them with excellence.

Would You help them stay focused on You and renew their strength when they grow weary?

Though their work may go on and on with no end in sight, may my children never consider giving up. Instead, I pray that they would enjoy the blessings and rewards You have for those who persist in doing good—eternal rewards as well as blessings in the here and now.

Amen.

Marriage

Then the LORD God said, "It is not good for the man to be alone. I will make a helper as his complement." . . . This is why a man leaves his father and mother and bonds with his wife, and they become one flesh.

GENESIS 2:18, 24

Giver of the Gift of Marriage,

Of the many influences that might affect my children's view of marriage, I pray that none would speak louder or be more cherished than Your Holy Word. May my children trust that You alone, who designed the gift of marriage, can adequately speak to what marriage should look like.

In time, after seeking Your heart and will, my children may find ones You would have them marry. If this happens, I pray that each of them would dig deep into Your Word to find out what You have to say about love, commitment, submission, and purity.

If marriage is in Your will for my children, may they find great joy and the richest blessings from Your hand.

Amen.

Comfort

Praise the God and Father of our Lord Jesus Christ,
the Father of mercies and the God of all comfort.
He comforts us in all our affliction, so that we may
be able to comfort those who are in any kind of affliction,
through the comfort we ourselves receive from God.

2 CORINTHIANS 1:3-4

Our Comforter,

I know You will lead my children through some dark days and hard times in this life. No matter their circumstances, I pray that they would experience Your closeness and comfort in these seasons.

You are such an amazing Redeemer. You take the difficult things we face and bring good from them. Bless You for Your goodness.

May my children learn precious truths about You as You comfort them in the valleys of life. And I pray that one day they would share these truths with others facing similar situations.

Amen.

Gratitude

Giving thanks always for everything
to God the Father
in the name of our Lord Jesus Christ.

EPHESIANS 5:20

Gracious God,

I ask today that my children would always have spirits of thanksgiving. May they realize that every good and perfect thing in their lives has come from You. Every friendship, every blue sky, and even every heartbeat is a gift from You.

I pray that they would never embrace a spirit of entitlement or haughty thoughts of deserving more, but may they live with a daily awareness of Your lavish provision.

May gratitude find regular expression in their prayers and what they say about You.

Amen.

Reverence

You must keep My Sabbaths
and revere My sanctuary;
I am Yahweh.

LEVITICUS 19:30

Holy King,

I pray that my children's lives would reflect a deep reverence for You. May they esteem and honor Your name and never consider using it in a way that dishonors You.

Give them such a great respect for Your Book that they will never treat it lightly or mishandle it. I pray that they would revere every day of the week as a holy gift from You and respect Sunday as a day of rest that You have ordained.

May they respect the place where Your people gather to worship, as well as the men and women who serve You in ministry.

Amen.

Patience

The fruit of the Spirit is . . . patience.

GALATIANS 5:22

God Who Is Slow to Anger,

In a society that seems to desire everything instantly, instill in my children a slow and steady calmness. May they be sure of who You are and certain that every promise in Your Word will be perfectly fulfilled. I pray that they would rest in Your sovereignty and wait patiently for You.

I know my children will become frustrated with their limitations at some point in their lives and will be tempted to lose patience. They may even have to endure some painful seasons that seem to go on for an unreasonable length of time.

In these times, I ask that You would help them patiently endure. May they not grow weary but calmly accept where You have them. May they patiently and faithfully serve You throughout their lives and trust You for the results.

Amen.

Thought Life

Whatever is true, whatever is honorable,
whatever is just, whatever is pure, whatever is lovely,
whatever is commendable—if there is any moral excellence
and if there is any praise—dwell on these things.

PHILIPPIANS 4:8

Holy One,

I pray that my children would take seriously Your command to guard their minds. Whatever they think about will surely find expression in their words and actions.

May they be wise and diligent regarding the forms of media they consume. Protect their eyes, ears, and minds from harmful images and content. With great intentionality, may they gravitate toward things that are respectable, pure, excellent, and right.

I pray that You would fix their thoughts on those things that honor and please You. May this not only result in good mental and psychological health but also lead to excellence and fruitfulness in serving You.

Amen.

Community

*If either falls, his companion can lift him up; but pity
the one who falls without another to lift him up.*

ECCLESIASTES 4:10

Faithful Friend,

You created us not for isolation but rather that we might experience life in community. I pray that my children would have a number of true companions in life, the kind who encourage them and help them remain strong in their faith.

My children's stories will include some dark and difficult chapters. At times, they may even stumble and fall. In these dark seasons, I pray that their friends would help them to their feet and set them back on the right path. May they be blessed with godly and faithful friends.

I also pray that my children would lift up and encourage their friends in their hours of need. May a life of isolation never appeal to my children.

Amen.

Faith

Now to Him who is able to do above and beyond
all that we ask or think according to
the power that works in us.

EPHESIANS 3:20

Almighty One,

On many days and in many ways, I have prayed for my children to have faith. I come today asking that they would not simply trust in You but would pray for incredible things in Your name for Your glory. May my children be so convinced of Your almighty power and the possibility of miracles that they would dare to pray for great things that only You can do.

May they boldly ask You to heal. May they ask You to make a way where there is no way. May they pray that You would change a heart.

Would You allow my children to have great confidence that with You not only are all things possible but nothing is ever impossible?

Amen.

Compassion

When [Jesus] saw the crowds,
He felt compassion for them,
because they were weary and worn out,
like sheep without a shepherd.

MATTHEW 9:36

Searching Shepherd,

Sometimes in my children's lives, those who don't trust in You will cause them great anger and frustration. In those moments, will You meet my children with the insight that these people are simply behaving in ways that are consistent with their unredeemed nature?

May my children's spirits be tender toward those sheep who have no Shepherd. I pray that You would move my children with compassion for them.

Would You give my children a heart for those who don't know You yet? Help them see unbelievers through Your eyes and realize that many of them are searching for meaning, truth, and You.

Amen.

Love

Dear friends, if God loved us in this [sacrificial]
way, we also must love one another.

1 JOHN 4:11

Loving Father,

Your great love for us is expressed in so many ways that are beyond our ability to even imagine. Yet the clearest expression of that love was giving Your only Son to save us.

I pray that my children, and all believers, would experience Your sacrificial love on Calvary as the redefining moment of their lifetimes.

May my children express their love for others by willingly sacrificing their desires, wants, and rights. Would You free my children from pride so their love would truly be a reflection of Your love?

Amen.

Speech

No foul language is to come from your mouth,
but only what is good for building up someone in
need, so that it gives grace to those who hear.

EPHESIANS 4:29

Word of Life,

I have often prayed that foul language would not flow from the lips of my children. Today, Lord, I ask that they would be quick to speak Your life-giving words to others.

Would You bless my children with the gift of being able to recall the right verse in the right situation? Those who do this well often have a powerful and holy influence in the lives of others.

I pray that You would give my children an eagerness to memorize Your Word and truly hide it in their hearts. May it beautifully flow from their lips to build up and encourage others.

Amen.

Parenting: Teaching by Example

Imitate me, as I also imitate Christ.

1 CORINTHIANS 11:1

Holy One,

It is my prayer and heart's desire to be holy like You, as You have called me to be.

It is a sobering thing to realize that when it comes to my children and their faith, so much more will be *caught* from me than *taught* by me.

Father, I want to live a life that sets a godly example for my children. May I passionately pursue Your heart and mind and exhibit a deep love of Your Word. I ask that my worship would be filled with spirit and truth and that I would joyfully serve fellow believers in the church and people of the world.

Remind me today that my actions have consequences. May I never do anything that might be a stumbling block to my children's faith.

I declare my ongoing need for Your daily grace, wisdom, and strength. Would You help my children follow my example as You help me follow You?

Amen.

Stumbling Block

Do not cause anyone to stumble.

1 CORINTHIANS 10:32, NIV

Holy One,

I pray that throughout their lives, my children will respect and look up to older believers as spiritual mentors. May these people realize the important roles they play in the lives of younger believers. Help them avoid compromises and failures that could damage their example and cause others, including my children, to stumble.

Likewise, I pray that my children's actions would never be a stumbling block to someone else. May they never say or do anything that would hinder a nonbeliever from coming to You.

May my children be willing to set aside their liberty if it might cause a weaker believer to stumble.

Amen.

God's Word

*Your decrees are my delight
and my counselors.*

PSALM 119:24

Wonderful Counselor,

Many people will speak into my children's lives—parents, extended family, neighbors, friends of the family, ministers, teachers, coaches, and guidance counselors—in addition to all they will absorb through media.

Many of these voices will give good advice, but I pray that my children would not trust in any of them like they trust in the counsel of Your Word.

Your wisdom, Lord, surpasses the best and highest thoughts of anyone else.

Amen.

Persecution

Those who are persecuted for righteousness are blessed,
for the kingdom of heaven is theirs.

MATTHEW 5:10

Jesus the Crucified,

If my children live as I have prayed they will, their righteousness and faith in You will likely offend people they meet along the way. Whatever the reason—refusing to cheat or join in a compromise, speaking the truth in love, or obeying Your Word—at some point, some people will dislike or even hate them.

They may know people who speak ill of them behind their backs or to their faces. They may even encounter direct physical confrontation. Would You meet them and protect them in those times? Would You give them strength, comfort, and peace to endure and stand strong in spite of persecution?

May opposition not discourage them but rather encourage them in the knowledge that their lives honor and glorify You. Please guide, bless, and take care of my children.

Amen.

Our Home

I will both lie down and sleep in peace,
for You alone, LORD, make me live in safety.

PSALM 4:8

Prince of Peace,

I lift up to You the times my children will spend in their rooms. May all the things they do in there—read, play, daydream, listen to music, do schoolwork, spend time with friends—be honoring to You.

I invite You to be Lord over all conversations that will happen within those walls. Please turn them away from wrong and dishonoring topics and keep them focused on what is holy and pure. May their rooms be safe, peaceful places for my children to grow into who You are making them to be.

At the end of every day, may they lie down and sleep in peace with their work and concerns attended to and set aside for the night. Please guide their thoughts as they lie in bed, look back on the day, and look ahead in anticipation. Please meet and lead them in those moments.

Amen.

Habits

*"Everything is permissible for me," but not everything
is helpful. "Everything is permissible for me," but
I will not be brought under the control of anything.*

1 CORINTHIANS 6:12

God of Freedom,

We live in a world of excess. Many things are good in moderation, but some people will take them to extremes. Spiritual bondage is most often the result of this.

I pray that my children would submit their desires and passions to You, inviting You to be Lord over those (and all) areas of their lives. May they be cautiously mindful of letting even small patterns develop into enslaving habits.

May they walk in freedom with You.

Amen.

Hope

Christ in you, the hope of glory.

COLOSSIANS 1:27

Our Unfailing Hope,

What a marvelous, incomprehensible truth that You would send Your Spirit to dwell within Your children. What a secure and unshakable foundation for our hope to be built upon. Those in this world who put their hope in anyone or anything else will ultimately be disappointed.

I pray that hope would always be strong and vibrant within my children. Even as they face times of frustration and discouragement, would You remind them that You have good things ahead for them? May this hope be an anchor that keeps them from drifting into depression or despair.

May Your Word and their worship always stir the flame of hope within them.

Amen.

Discipline

Do not despise the LORD's instruction, my son,
and do not loathe His discipline;
for the LORD disciplines the one He loves,
just as a father, the son he delights in.

PROVERBS 3:11-12

Perfect Father,

As my children grow, there will be times when You will discipline them to provide correction and instruction. I know that this may involve suffering and consequences.

I pray that my children would not despise Your discipline but would be quick to learn from it as they cry out to You.

Even during the most difficult days, may they never question Your love for them but find comfort in knowing that You are perfect in all Your ways, and You discipline those You love. Would You help them see that You always lead us along paths that will grow our faith and increase our wisdom and blessings?

May Your discipline in their lives produce much fruit for Your glory. Please help them endure it well.

Amen.

Growing in Wisdom

Jesus increased in wisdom.

LUKE 2:52

Wise One,

I pray that my children would be blessed with a passionate desire to learn. Would You give them sharp minds and diligent spirits to increase in wisdom as Jesus did?

May the process of receiving instruction be a joyful experience for my children. Turn them away from laziness and motivate them to press on with their education.

May their quest for wisdom be more than simply gaining knowledge. Please grow within them a deep hunger for the eternal truths of Your Word.

Amen.

Peace

The fruit of the Spirit is . . . peace.

GALATIANS 5:22

Prince of Peace,

Simply knowing You produces peace in the hearts of Your children. What a calming truth it is that the almighty King and Creator of the universe has accepted us through our faith in Your sacrificial death.

Our peace rests in Your character. May this be the foundation of peace in my children's lives. I pray that even amid the storms of life, they would be so confident in Your sovereignty that their spirits would know all is well.

May this peace—the fruit of Your Spirit—conquer all their fears and doubts.

Amen.

Love

God's love was revealed among us in this way:
God sent His One and Only Son into the world
so that we might live through Him.

1 JOHN 4:9

God Who Is Love,

Your love is expressed to us in countless ways every moment, but none of them is greater than the fact that You sent Your Son to be our Savior.

This time of year, when the sights and sounds of the holiday bombard us from all angles, I pray that my children would hear this message above all: *You love them!*

May everything about this season of celebration bring to their minds that You took the initiative, You pursued them, You desire a relationship with them, and You made a way for that to happen.

We are amazed.

Amen.

Influence

The one who loves a pure heart
and gracious lips—the king is his friend.

PROVERBS 22:11

God of Truth and Wisdom,

You make clear to us that our lips simply express what is already in our hearts. I pray that pure love, worship, grace, and wisdom would overflow from my children.

As a result, may they have an amazing, redemptive influence on the people around them. Would You use them powerfully in the lives of others and even grant them access to and favor with those who have a far greater influence in this world?

Amen.

Greed

Be on guard against all greed because one's life
is not in the abundance of his possessions.

LUKE 12:15

God of Heavenly Riches,

The desire for more material possessions is woven into the fabric of many TV, magazine, and radio advertisement we encounter. All too often, the result of casually walking in the mall and window-shopping is that we become discontent with what we already have and want something new instead.

Lord, I know that the spirit of materialism will try to get its hooks into my children's hearts, but I ask that You would thwart these attacks. May my children live in freedom and refuse to be caught in a pattern of coveting. Would You help them see that real riches are found in relationships, not in material things?

When they have a choice between striving for spiritual blessing and pursuing material blessing, may they choose what really satisfies and endures.

Amen.

Character of God: Sovereign

We know that all things work together
for the good of those who love God:
those who are called according to His purpose.

ROMANS 8:28

Sovereign King,

I pray that the promise of today's verse will bring glorious and holy hope to the hearts of my children. May they have great confidence that You work through *all things*, not just the good things that happen in life, for Your glory and for their ultimate good.

In some of the darker and harder times of their lives—suffering, temptation, loss, sin, failure, heartbreak, disappointment—may the truth of Your sovereignty be a precious pearl my children will cling to. I pray that they would find great hope, comfort, and encouragement in knowing that You are in control.

Amen.

Obedience

Children, obey your parents in everything,
for this pleases the Lord.

COLOSSIANS 3:20

Our Perfect Father,

You do not delight in our outward conformity to Your will if our hearts are not set on doing what is right. Performing this kind of obedience is like being a rebellious child who reluctantly complies with a parent's instruction to sit down. With a defiant look, the child exclaims, "I may be sitting in this chair, but in my heart I'm still standing!"

I pray that such a spirit of rebellion and pride would not take root in my children. Lord, if any seeds of pride fall upon their hearts, may they simply not provide the soil for them to grow. May my children willingly obey instruction with attitudes of love, submission, and trust. I pray that this spirit would characterize my children's relationships with me, just as I desire for it to characterize my relationship with You.

Would You give them great joy in knowing this pleases You?

Amen.

Integrity

Let your word "yes" be "yes," and your "no" be "no."
Anything more than this is from the evil one.

MATTHEW 5:37

Righteous Judge,

I pray that my children's integrity would speak so loudly that their words can be few. May the words they do speak be proved honest and right.

Please guide me in teaching them to be people who do what they say they will do. May my children never be known as promise breakers.

Bless them with sterling reputations, and may they never need to resort to swearing an oath to convince others of their integrity.

Amen.

Sharing

Don't neglect to do what is good and to share,
for God is pleased with such sacrifices.

HEBREWS 13:16

Our Generous God,

I ask that my children would believe that every good thing they have is a gift from You. May they learn to hold their possessions loosely, trusting that You can always provide more.

I pray that my children would reflect Your generous heart in the way they handle things that belong to them. May they be unselfish and willing to share sacrificially, especially with their siblings.

Give them a passion to please You in this way.

Amen.

Anticipating Jesus' Return

*This Jesus, who has been taken from you
into heaven, will come in the same way that
you have seen Him going into heaven.*

ACTS 1:11

God Who Is Faithful to Return,

This season of the year is such a time of anticipation, especially for children. They can't wait to get out of school, take part in holiday traditions, and most of all open presents!

Our family also loves singing hymns like "O Come, O Come, Emmanuel" and "Come, Thou Long-Expected Jesus" that reflect our longing to see You in Your incarnation.

I pray that my children will always live with a sweet anticipation of Your return to earth. May they live with a sure faith and confidence that You will keep Your promise to return again—this time not as a humble baby but as the reigning, mighty King of kings and Lord of lords.

Amen.

Growing Spiritually

*Like newborn infants, desire the pure spiritual
milk, so that you may grow by it.*

1 PETER 2:2

God Who Leads Us Onward,

I pray that my children would have an enormous appetite for Your Word. May their love for and delight in Your truth be evident to those around them.

I ask that this would be a relentless passion in every season of their lives. May they always seek out excellent teaching of Your truth. Would You guide them to solid Bible-believing churches and ministries that can help them grow spiritually?

When they are young, help them feed on the "pure spiritual milk" of Your Word. As they grow and mature in their faith, may they never be satisfied with light topical talks about spiritual things but always crave the meat of Your Holy Word.

Amen.

Generosity

Each person should do as he has decided
in his heart—not reluctantly or out of necessity,
for God loves a cheerful giver.

2 CORINTHIANS 9:7

Lavish Giver of Grace and Every Blessing,

You know that my desire is for my children to live with open hands, not clutching or clinging to anything You have given them but willing to pass it on as a blessing to others.

May my children find it a joyous privilege to give to You. Would You give them the ability to be spontaneous givers? But more importantly, may their giving be planned and systematic, never grudging or sporadic.

May they always know thc incredible richness of being channels of Your blessings.

Amen.

God with Us

See, the virgin will become pregnant
and give birth to a son,
and they will name Him Immanuel,
which is translated "God is with us."

MATTHEW 1:23

Our Ever-Present Savior,

I ask that Your name, Immanuel, would deeply impact the lives of my children.

May they

- always be in wonder that You took the initiative and came to earth to redeem us;
- find great comfort in Your presence during the most difficult, sad, or frightening times of their lives;
- know the peace found in Your nearness in times of failure;
- experience courage knowing that You are with them as they step into the unknown; and
- find Your closeness challenging them to live soberly as they face times of temptation.

We bless You, Jesus, for being with us!

Amen.

Joy

Rejoice in the Lord always.
I will say it again: Rejoice!

PHILIPPIANS 4:4

God of Joy,

Since Your Word repeatedly commands us to be joyful, our assumption is that You understand well that it is not always easy. Joy must be more than an emotion since You wouldn't command us to feel a feeling!

I pray that my children would know lasting joy—the confidence that You are in control of everything and are working for their good and Your glory. May this truth produce in their souls an abiding sense of peace and hopefulness that no circumstance can shake.

Would You continually fill them with Your true joy?

Amen.

Gratitude

*Giving thanks always for everything
to God the Father
in the name of our Lord Jesus Christ.*

EPHESIANS 5:20

Gift of God,

I ask that my children's hearts would be gardens of gratitude where many other virtues will grow and bear fruit. May my children be thankful for every gift, blessing, and good thing that comes from Your hand.

I also pray that they would be thankful for blessings and victories that are yet to come. At times when they feel stuck and are seeking Your direction, may their confidence in Your goodness cause them to express their gratitude to You in advance as they anticipate Your answer to their prayers.

As my children grow, Lord, I pray that You would enable them to do the hardest thing: express thankfulness to You in the midst of pain, trial, persecution, or testing. This can only come from a heart that is consumed with the glory of who You are.

I want that for my children.

Amen.

Christmas

Today a Savior, who is Messiah the Lord,
was born for you in the city of David.

LUKE 2:11

Most High God,

Thank You for this blessed day of celebration!

This day, and the season that surrounds it, is filled with many good things. Yet I pray that our family would find creative ways to keep our hearts focused on the heart of this holiday.

You saw our great need. You solved our greatest problem. You provided what we were helpless to provide for ourselves.

You sent us a Savior!

May my children, and our whole family, express our gratitude and bless You today for the gift of Your Son, Jesus.

Amen.

Siblings

Do nothing out of rivalry or conceit, but in humility
consider others as more important than yourselves.

PHILIPPIANS 2:3

Servant of God,

It's easy for two proud people to exchange angry words and engage in aggressive actions, but between two humble people it's almost impossible.

I pray today that my children would, in a healthy and holy way, truly consider the needs of others as more important than their own. Help me model for them this mindset—a mindset which, it seems to me, is at the heart of being able to overcome selfishness, pride, and conceit (in other words, all the things that can cause conflict in their relationships with You, me, and everyone else).

Even today, may an attitude of humble selflessness be evident in my children's relationships with their siblings. I ask that You would bless us with a home where thoughtfulness, kindness, concern, sharing, and love are lived out daily. What a delightful life that would be! Please help us.

Amen.

Looking Ahead

Forgetting what is behind and reaching forward
to what is ahead, I pursue as my goal the prize
promised by God's heavenly call in Christ Jesus.

PHILIPPIANS 3:13-14

God of Our Tomorrows,

I pray that my children would live with their eyes fixed on what's ahead. May they be so certain that Your mercy and grace have covered all their sins and mistakes that grudges, bitterness, failures, or missed opportunities of the past won't bind or hinder them.

Would You keep them from looking back over their shoulders, even when they succeed? I pray that they would not focus on achievements, virtuous deeds, or accomplishments of the past but see these simply as offerings already laid at Your feet.

May they never define themselves by past victories or past failures.

Amen.

Walking in Truth

I have no greater joy than this:
to hear that my children are walking in the truth.

3 JOHN 1:4

Living God,

This year, I have often asked that Your Word would occupy a place of great importance in the lives of my children. I pray about this so much because I truly believe it is the pathway to salvation for them.

I want them to love, believe, and obey Your Word—not just now and not simply for a season of their lives. No, I ask that this would be an enduring pattern throughout their lifetimes.

For Your great glory, now and forevermore.

Amen.

Path of Life

He leads me along the right paths
for His name's sake.

PSALM 23:3

Shepherd,

It is easy to trust You with my children. You are perfect in all Your ways. Your love for each of us, including my children, is incomprehensible. You are faithful to provide, protect, and care for each of us.

As my children look to the seasons of life and years ahead, may they have confidence that Your hand is upon them and actively leading them. It gives me great peace to know that if they are seeking You, You will lead them in paths of righteousness.

My greatest joy will be to watch Your plan, purpose, and pathway unfold in their lives.

Amen.

Parenting:
Releasing My Children

For this boy I prayed, and the LORD
has granted me my request which I asked of Him.
So I have also dedicated him to the LORD; as long
as he lives he is dedicated to the LORD.

1 SAMUEL 1:27-28, NASB

Gracious Giver,

Even now, I can recall the overwhelming joy I felt the first time I held each of my children—life-changing gifts from You. For all the incredible, joyous moments of being a parent, there will also be some really difficult ones. Many of these moments will require letting go in some heartrending way.

Each moment of letting go, whether big or small, will call me to trust You. Whether it's the first time my children have a babysitter, the first day of kindergarten or high school, out-of-town trips, mission trips, college, or marriage, these moments will stir up intense emotions for me as a parent.

Yet through it all, I will look to You and rest in knowing that You love my children even more than I do. Your love is deeper, higher, wider, more lasting, and more perfect. You are fully able to protect and keep them safe in Your hand. My peace is in Your sovereignty. I will rest in who You are. Help me release them well as I entrust them to You.

Thank You for Your great love for my children.

Amen.

Parenting:
My Children's Legacy

From eternity to eternity
the LORD's faithful love is toward those who fear Him,
and His righteousness toward the grandchildren
of those who keep His covenant,
who remember to observe His precepts.

PSALM 103:17-18

Father,

I come to You at a time when many reflect on the events of the past year and look ahead as a new year unfolds. I find myself doing both today. I am so aware of Your goodness and mercy leading up to this moment in my family tree. You have pursued me, called me to Yourself, and granted me faith to trust in You.

I know You also have great plans for my children and have heard me pour out my petitions on their behalf.

With all the good, right, and holy things I desire for them, I also want these things for my children's children, should You choose to bless my children with families of their own. I want all of us to be part of a family legacy that brings great glory to You, our Redeemer. I want the generations that follow to know Your love and to walk closely with You.

May You be glorified forever!

Amen.

Index

About the Author

TONY WOOD is a multiple Gospel Music Association Dove Award winner as well as a nominee for Songwriter of the Year. He has written songs recorded by Michael W. Smith, Francesca Battistelli, Zach Williams, Matt Redman, for KING & COUNTRY, Big Daddy Weave, TobyMac, We Are Messengers, Point of Grace, 4Him, Mandisa, Jason Crabb, Kutless, Natalie Grant, Sandi Patty, Larnell Harris, Selah, Gaither Vocal Band, Steven Curtis Chapman, Mark Schultz, Kari Jobe, Reba McEntire, Ricky Skaggs, Oak Ridge Boys, and many others. Tony and his wife, Terri, are the parents of four daughters.

TONYWOODONLINE.COM

FOCUS ON THE FAMILY®

PARENTING HAS THOSE "WHAT NOW?" MOMENTS.

Even if it feels like you're standing at the edge of a tall cliff without a parachute — there is hope.

The **7 Traits of Effective Parenting** book by Dr. Danny Huerta unpacks the seven well-researched traits shared by effective parents.

Get your copy at
Store.FocusOnTheFamily.com

© 2023 Focus on the Family

CP1870

IT'S OFFICIAL:
Parenting Gen Z is super hard.

Gen Z is the most non-Christian generation in our history.

The culture is shifting faster than parents can keep up and any false step can shut the door on faith talks. This book will help you guide your Gen Z child through a bunch of topics, including:

Why faith?
Gaming limits
Depression
LGBQTIA
Sex/Porn

Order your copy!
Store.FocusOnTheFamily.com

FOCUS ON THE FAMILY®

CP1881